PALMYRA

By the same author

PETRA

PALMYRA

By

IAIN BROWNING

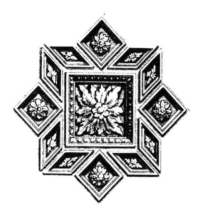

Noyes Press

Copyright © 1979 by Iain Browning
Library of Congress Catalog Card Number: 79–16591
ISBN: 0–8155–5054–5
Printed in Great Britain

Published in the United States by
NOYES PRESS
Noyes Building
Park Ridge, New Jersey 07656

Library of Congress Cataloging in Publication Data

Browning, Iain.
  Palmyra.

  Bibliography: p.
  Includes index.
    1. Palmyra, Syria.   I. Title.
DS99.P17B7   939'.4   79–16591
ISBN 0–8155–5054–5

To
Vern *and* Dorothy

Acknowledgements

It is with real pleasure that I acknowledge the help and encouragement given so freely to me by Denys and Sybille Haynes. Quite apart from the Preface with which Denys so handsomely opens this book, I am more than grateful for their ever-available guidance when I was writing the text: to have the attention and interest of scholars of their standing has been an invaluable asset.

Whilst writing this book I have been greatly assisted by many of my friends to all of whom I send my thanks. Especially my thanks go to Pierre Chary who translated for me, to Dr Dominique Collon who guided me through the Assyrian legal codes, whilst the kind hospitality of Lady Brunner when I visited Grey's Court is much appreciated. I should also like to thank Mr Geoffrey Wilkinson who coped most generously with my photographic problems.

I am much indebted to Mr & Mrs John Dawkins and to Mr Stephen Freer whose ancestor 'rescued' Palmyra and to the Duke of Wellington who not only permitted me to illustrate the ceiling in his Dining Room at Stratfield Saye but also kindly sent me a lengthy extract from his personal war diaries.

A special note, however, for Mr & Mrs Werner Viertmann whose involvement in this book started in Palmyra where they looked after me so gently and warmly, and whose interest has never failed. Also to Mr Barry Norman who gave a great deal of help in the preparation of the text, read proofs with me and undertook the laborious task of compiling the Index.

Earls Court,
London   IAIN BROWNING

Contents

Illustrations

The monochrome illustrations may be found
from the Index, where their page references
are set in italics.

COLOUR PLATES

MAPS

All illustrations in this book are by the author except for the following which are reproduced with
the kind permission of: Mr Stephen Freer, Fig. 24b; The Duke of Wellington, Fig. 36; Mr John
Dawkins and The University of Glasgow Art Gallery, Fig. 35; The National Portrait Gallery, Fig.
24a; The University of Amsterdam, Fig. 18; The Ny Carlsberg Glyptotek, Copenhagen, Figs. 5, 7
and 13; The Palestine Exploration Fund, Figs. 19, 58, 65, 73, 95, 101, 104 and 119; The Victoria
and Albert Museum, Fig. 37; The Trustees of the British Museum, Figs. 9, 10, 11 and 12; The
Trustees of the British Library, Figs. 20, 21, 22, 23, 26, 28, 38, 62, 69, 79, 93, 103, 122, 132, 135 and
138. Colour plates: Mr Werner Viertmann, Plate 4b.

Preface

DENYS L. HAYNES

'Rise up and go into the world to release it from error and send word to the Jinn that I give them leave to build Tadmor with hewn stones and columns.' So God to King Solomon, according to the pre-Islamic poet Al-Nabigha al-Dhubyain. Like the writers of 1 Kings and 2 Chronicles, the poet was mistaken in ascribing the foundation of Tadmor, the classical Palmyra, to Solomon; but who would blame him for suggesting that only a supernatural agency could have conjured up so magnificent a metropolis in the middle of the desert? 'I doubt whether any city in the world,' wrote Dr William Halifax on rediscovering the ruins of Palmyra in 1691, 'could have challenged precedence of this in its glory'; and even so sober and objective an historian as the great Rostovtzeff, who visited Palmyra by motor car shortly after the First World War, confessed to 'that same romantic enchantment which all previous travellers have experienced'.

Yet, for all its miraculous appearance, the spectacular development of Palmyra was solidly based on geographical and historical realities. Situated half-way between the Syrian coast and the valley of the Euphrates, the city rose at a point where the desert is rendered habitable and even, given careful irrigation, richly fertile by the abundant waters of the spring Efqa: still today the visitor may take his pick of more than twenty different kinds of date. Habitation of the oasis goes back to Neolithic times and the name Tadmor is attested in a 'Cappodocian' tablet as early as the nineteenth century B.C., by which time a town, or at least a large village, must have been established on the site. But it was not for another two millennia that the historical situation arose which allowed the oasis to develop an urban civilisation on the magnificent scale to which the remains bear witness. With the collapse of the Seleucid empire in 64 B.C. the rival mights of Rome and Parthia confronted one another across a turbulent, bandit-infested no-man's-land, in which the flourishing commerce established between East and West in Hellenistic times might well have bled to death, had not the inhabitants of Tadmor seen their opportunity and seized it. By organising a highly efficient corps of desert police, they created a safe route for caravans from Dura-Europus on the Euphrates to Damascus and Emesa in Syria and so attracted to themselves a major share of this oriental trade which steadily increased in volume under the Roman empire.

PREFACE

Known to the Romans as Palmyra (the place of palms), the oasis was early—and no doubt amicably—incorporated in the Roman province of Syria, probably in A.D. 17; but it continued to enjoy a considerable measure of independence, especially in the control of its desert army. Hadrian, who visited Palmyra in A.D. 129, granted it the rights of a free city and Septimius Severus raised it to the status of a Roman colony, a distinction which, in theory at least, put its citizens on the same level as those of Rome itself. But the underlying ambiguity of Palmyra's relationship to Rome revealed itself in the crisis resulting from the capture by the Persians of the emperor Valerian in A.D. 260. In this crisis a leading Palmyrene nobleman named Odenaethus came to the rescue by mobilising the city's desert army and inflicting a severe defeat on Sapur I, a success which he followed up by reconquering Mesopotamia for Rome. But when, after his suspiciously sudden death in A.D. 267, his widow Zenobia occupied Egypt and Asia Minor and claimed the title of Augustus for her infant son, Rome could no longer turn a blind eye to this open challenge to her sovereignty. Despatching Probus to recover Egypt, the emperor Aurelian himself led an expeditionary force through Asia Minor to Syria, where he defeated the main Palmyrene army at Antioch and Emesa and then laid siege to Palmyra, which capitulated. Zenobia, who had been caught while trying to escape to Persia, spent the rest of her days in comfortable retirement in a villa at Tibur; and her city, too, would have enjoyed the emperor's clemency, had it not massacred its Roman garrison shortly after his departure. The emperor returned and destroyed it (A.D. 273).

As we should expect from the city's history, the visible remains of Palmyra date for the most part from the first three centuries A.D., though there is evidence that monumental building had already begun, under the influence of the Hellenistic east, as early as the second half of the first century B.C. Of the surviving buildings the earliest and most imposing is the Temple of Bel dedicated in A.D. 32, a curious hybrid in which the forms of Romano–Syrian architecture are uneasily adapted to a plan dictated by the needs of an oriental cult. The slightly later Temple of Nabo, on the other hand, and the second-century Temple of Ba'alshamin are purely Romano–Syrian in type. The most striking feature of the city as a whole is the extent of its colonnaded streets. Such streets occur, of course, in several Roman provincial cities in the Near East and North Africa; but nowhere else do they play so dominant an architectural role as here. The long, basilica-like vistas created by these monumental thoroughfares must have largely concealed the individual buildings on either side of them. Beyond the city bounds extensive cemeteries witness to the importance which the Palmyrenes—a people of Aramaic origin but with a strong Arab admixture—attached to the afterlife. Of the funerary monuments the most conspicuous are the tower-tombs, but the complex and capacious hypogea are no less interesting. Both types of tomb are lavishly decorated internally, their ornament including carved stone portraits of the deceased in a hieratic, two-dimensional style which, unlike Palmyrene architecture, owes more to Parthia than to the classical world.

Few ancient sites could be more rewarding than Palmyra for the interested layman; and it is he, in particular, who will benefit from the present work which provides him with a much-needed companion and guide. Mr Browning is not an archaeologist by profession but he possesses an all-important quality which many professional archaeologists lack: a keen visual sensibility; and this, combined with a wide practical knowledge of architectural design and ornament, gives his work its special value and authenticity. Moreover, he draws very well, as many vivid reconstructions attest, and he is an excellent photographer. I am confident that this new work will enjoy as great a success as his previous work on Petra.

Denys L. Haynes

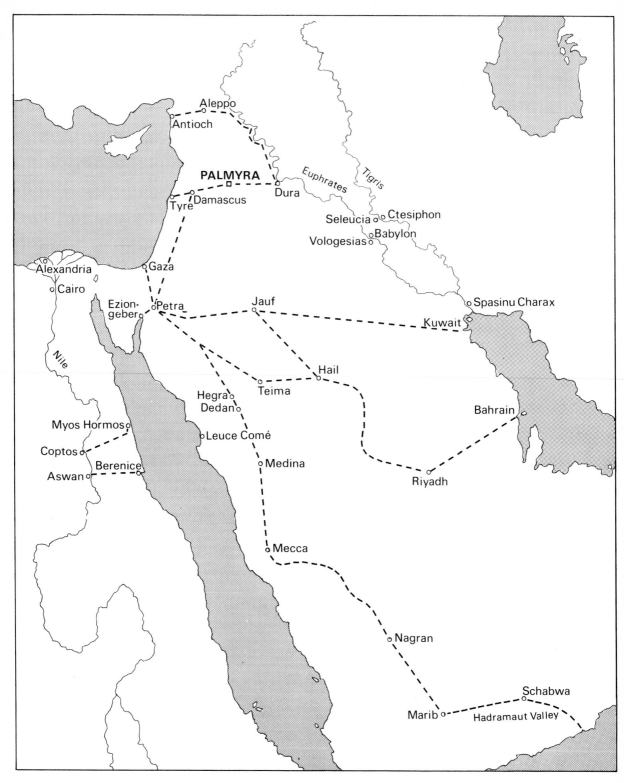

Map 1 Trade routes of the ancient Middle East.

CHAPTER ONE

The Bride of the Desert

PALMYRA is well named 'The Bride of the Desert'. If any city of the ancient world was wedded to the desert it must surely have been this remarkable metropolis. Palmyra lies some 230 kilometres north-east of Damascus on the ancient trade route between Homs (ancient Emesa) and Dura-Europos on the banks of the Euphrates. Between Homs and Palmyra it is not so much a desert as a sparsely inhabited steppe, but eastwards and southwards lie the vast horizons of the Syrian desert in all its intimidating ferocity. The site is well protected on two sides by high, bleak hills which provide a dramatic backdrop to the present-day ruins. To the north the Gebel Hayane, Gebel el Tarr and Gebel Mohammed ibn Ali seem to rise like huge static waves, lapping the bastions of the city. To the east and south the desert slips away into hot, quivering nothingness, open to the wide skies with the silvery strip of a salt lake in the Wadi Miyah glinting like a mirage below the hazy horizon.

Across the eastern desert lies the Euphrates which, having linked with the Tigris, comes out into the Persian Gulf. From there the traders of the ancient worlds had access to the Indian Ocean and all the markets of the east. Trading vessels could navigate right up the Euphrates as far as Dura-Europos—indeed beyond. From Dura it was a short cut across the desert to the great emporia cities of the Levant via Palmyra.

This route was by no means the only one in the ancient Middle East: much depended on the international political situation at a given time as to which passage was taken. This aspect will be more fully explored in the next chapter, but here it is worth looking at the network of routes which existed (Map 1).

Well into the first millennium B.C. the eastern Mediterranean was waking up to the comforts which civilisation could provide and there was a demand for luxury goods. The majority of these were imported, often from far afield. By the first century A.D. goods were being received from as far away as China. Merchandise from the Orient would probably have come by coaster up through the Straits of Homuz and into the Persian Gulf. On entering the delta of the Tigris/Euphrates the ships would head for Spasinu Charax. From there the route was up the Euphrates, or Tigris, to one of the ancient cities of Mesopotamia such as Babylon,

Ctesiphon and Seleucia. After that the merchants could choose which way to go. One route, which cannot have been much favoured because of the enormous leap required across the top of the Nejd and Nefud deserts, went direct to the emporium city of Petra, possibly via Jauf. Other routes across the top of the Arabian peninsula were from Kuwait or Bahrain which traversed the deserts by either Jauf or the ancient city of Teima. An important amount of traffic at one time was routed south before entering the Straits of Homuz and might be landed at the mouth of the Hadramaut after which the goods were taken on the long over-land trek up through the western chain of mountains via Schabwa, Marib, Nagran, Mecca, Medina and so northwards to Petra. Alternatively the vessels could navigate right round the south of Arabia, going through the Straits of Bab el Mandeb and up the coast to the Gulf of Aqaba port of Ezion-Geber. From there it was only a short land route up to the Nabatean capital. All these Arabian routes went via Petra, whence they reached the Levantine entrepôts of Damascus, Tyre and Gaza.

The most northern route, over the top of the Syrian desert, clinging closely to the fringe of the Fertile Crescent was from Dura on the Euphrates, up to Thapsacus, to Aleppo and thence to Antioch.

This tangle of routes allowed a variety of passages, but often enough powerful nations would channel the trade through territories they controlled because there were valuable revenues to be had from it. Not that merchants necessarily objected to this, for with the revenues they paid generally came the advantage of a safe transit along well policed routes. It was no business of the merchants to become involved in politics; all they wanted was to be allowed to pursue their trade without hindrance.

With the collapse of the Nabatean Empire in A.D. 106, the emphasis shifted to the northern trade routes. This, and the balance of power between Rome and Parthia, was the springboard for Palmyra's meteoric and spectacular rise to fortune.

There was a settlement at Palmyra as early as the second millennium B.C., though only on a tiny scale. Even before this there is evidence of nomadic or seasonal use of the site. But by the first century A.D. small objects found in burials tell us that importation and trading were taking place—possibly on quite a considerable scale. This is supported by the fact that the oasis was developing into an appreciable urban settlement. Indeed, an inscription dated 44 B.C., the earliest known Palmyrene inscription, establishes that there were 'monumental' buildings on the site. To be able to build in such a way indicates that the town was drawing revenues from somewhere or other. They are unlikely to have been derived from local natural resources; more probably they came from a well organised and established trade practice with its attendant tariffs.

We do not know when an organised trading establishment was first set up in

Palmyra. It is unlikely that formal trading facilities and caravanserai were provided by the local inhabitants in the early days. But with vastly improved communications and the provision of services, the settlement grew into an emporium of increasing importance which led to fame and fortune in the second and third centuries A.D.

From that period of great prosperity we have an almost unique record of the goods passing through Palmyra. Not all these goods were in transit for, as the merchants grew rich, so they became consumers. The so-called Palmyrene Tariff is a large stone slab or stele, measuring 1 metre 75 high by 4 metres 80 wide, upon which is inscribed the longest known text in the Palmyrene dialect of Aramaean. This is backed up with the same text in Greek. The stele is dated A.D. 137 and records a collection of old and new financial laws and taxes. The text was published by the Russian Prince Abamelek Lazareff with the aid of V. V. Latysheff, the Marquis de Vogüé and Professor H. Dessau. The stele itself was, through the efforts of the Prince and the former Russian Archaeological Institute in Istanbul, removed from Palmyra and taken to the Hermitage Museum in Leningrad, where it now rests.

The stele is badly worn in places with some sections of the text completely obliterated. But it is possible to put together the majority of the inscription, using both the Palmyrene and Greek texts. The preamble seeks to codify old fiscal and other laws previously based on custom. Then follow the various individual clauses of the Tariff.

Clause I   *Slaves*

About those who send slaves to Palmyra or its territories, the publican will take for each individual — 22 denarii

For the slave who is sold in Town but who is not sent away — 12 d

For a senior slave who is sold — 10 d

If the buyer exports the slaves, he will give for each individual — 12 d

Clause II   *Dry Goods*

The publican will collect per camel load of dry goods going into Palmyra and its territories, per camel load — 3 d

Per camel load at the entrance — 3 d

Per donkey load at the entrance and at the exit — 2 d

Clause III   *Purple*

For the wool dyed purple, for each fleece imported and exported — 8 d

Clause IV *Perfumes*

Per camel load of aromatic oil which is brought in in alabaster (bottles or jars)	25 d
And of what is afterwards sold of that oil, at the entrance, per camel load	13 d
Per camel load of aromatic oil which is brought in in goatskin bottles, at the entrance	13 d
and at the exit	7 d
Per donkey load of aromatic oil which is brought in in alabaster, at the entrance	13 d
and at the exit	7 d
Per donkey load of aromatic oil which is brought in in goatskin bottles, at the entrance	7 d
and at the exit	4 d

Perfumes were one of the principal objects of Palmyrene commerce and as such commanded a high tax. It can be seen that the perfumes of high quality were carried in alabaster jars whereas the more common and less expensive oils travelled in skin bottles.

Clause V deals with oils, by which is meant olive oil. The next four clauses deal with various fats, beasts of burden, salted goods such as the dried fish from Lake Tiberias in Palestine which was considered a great delicacy, and cattle. After an additional tax on the sellers of perfume in Clause X, we come to a tax on prostitutes.

Clause XI *Prostitutes*

Also, the publican will collect from prostitutes, from the one who charges 1 d or more he will collect 1 d, from the one who charges 8 As he will collect 8 As and from the one who charges 6 As, 6 As and so on.

This was probably a monthly tax based on the Roman principle set up by Caligula (A.D. 37–41), i.e. the monthly tax levied on a prostitute was the same sum as she charged for one act.

Clause XII concerns other professional taxes of which the most interesting is on cloth merchants who were 'in Town'. It indicates that, as traders find today, there were peak and low periods in business. The tax on Palmyrene cloth merchants varied. This was probably in proportion to the activity of their trade which fluctuated according to the seasons and according to the number of foreigners and tribesmen in town.

Clause XIII   *Water Rates*

For the use of both springs of water which are in the town   800 d

This seems, at first glance, an exorbitant tax but it probably meant that a merchant could buy for this figure an abonnement which entitled him, amongst other things, to water his camels at any time. When one considers that a well organised caravan could number up to a thousand camels the charge seems pretty reasonable. Water was the most valuable of Palmyra's assets.

The next two clauses deal with agricultural produce and unladen beasts of burden, whilst Clause XVI constitutes the preamble to the New Laws of Palmyra.

Then follow various clauses dealing with domestic produce including salt (Clause XVII), a further piece of legislation on courtesans and a tax on greases.

Clause XXVI   *Statues*

It has been decided that bronze pictures and statues should be taxed as bronze. One statue will be taxed as half a load, and two statues as a full load.

A camel load has been calculated* to be in the region of 200 kilos. 'Bronze pictures' evidently refers to bronze reliefs.

Clause XXVII   *Salt*

It seemed a good thing that salt should be sold on the main square where gatherings take place. The Palmyrene who buys salt for his own use will pay 1 Italic As per modius. The existing tax on salt (Clause XVII) in Palmyra shall be estimated, as in the province, on the As, and the salt shall be delivered to the merchants to be sold according to the custom.

These two clauses were probably aimed at protecting and fostering the use and trade in salt produced locally. Salt in a hot climate is, of course, vital to life and so some regulation would have been necessary in an organised society. The Senate also felt that it was right that the State should derive some benefit from such an important item and levied a selling tax on the 'farmer'.

The final clause deals again with cattle regulations and stipulations.

The Publican referred to in the Tariff was the official nominated by the Senate to collect the various taxes. An 'As' was a Roman copper coin, originally weighing 12 ounces but finally reduced to ½ an ounce; the reference in Clause XXVII to an Italic As denotes its Roman origin. In the same clause the word 'modius' refers to the Roman measure.

From the Tariff we have a very clear picture of the commodities which flowed through Palmyra at that time. Excavations have shown that other items were also

* J.–B. Chabot: *Choix d'Inscriptions de Palmyre*, Paris 1922.

imported such as silk yarn and jade from China, muslin, spices, ebony, myrrh, ivory, pearls and precious stones. Pottery was an early import but this trade to all intents and purposes ceased after the first century A.D. when local industry seems to have been able to cope with the demand. However, wares from the Eastern Mediterranean, probably from the Antioch area, continued to come through, presumably because of their beauty and variety. The distinctive green glaze pottery of Mesopotamia has also been found, betokening a strong eastern supply. Glass, however, was imported from Syria. Jewellery materials have also been found. Along with perfumes, one can see that it was essentially a luxury trade.

The Syrians have been called the middlemen of antiquity. In Robin Fedden's words, 'at this period (they) filled a role that in later Middle Ages was to fall to Venice. Their vessels went everywhere and the cunning Syro-Phoenician banker merchants were familiar figures in the Markets of the West. The Latin Roman did not altogether care for the vulgar wealth and monopolising efficiency of these people, and by the first century A.D. there was room for Juvenal's famous complaint about the Orontes encroaching on the Tiber: Syrus in Tiberim defluxit Orontes. The encroachment, however, continued.'* There was a Palmyrene merchant community domiciled in Dura-Europos and in Rome with their own temple outside the Porta Portuensis. Whilst the Seleucid Empire existed they had their representatives in Seleucia on the Tigris who were later transferred to Vologasias when the Parthians founded this rival city. From there the Palmyrenes penetrated down to Spasinu Charax; indeed it was through a Palmyrene emissary, one Alexandros, that the Emperor Germanicus in A.D. 18 sent a message to Mesene, 'King' of that area. In fact Palmyrenes were, rather suddenly, everywhere.

Trade was everything to the Palmyrenes. It was their business acumen and courage as traders which brought them and their city such vast wealth and prosperity. Certainly throughout the first century, the proceeds of this trade were shared out between individual merchants and the city, the latter taking its share in the form of clearly regulated taxes. The city encouraged success and publicly honoured it.

Even before Palmyra was launched on her headlong, though short, period of splendour, she had been making her presence felt. There must have been a feeling in the air that something was going to happen, for when the time came the Palmyrenes were ready with their stations and representatives abroad and with a practical and welcoming organisation at home amongst the palms.

* Robin Fedden: *Syria and Lebanon.*

CHAPTER TWO

People, Power and Politics

THE area in and around Palmyra was inhabited by man in pre-historic times. The excavations of the University of Tokyo under the direction of Dr Takeru Akazawa at the Doura Cave, east of Palmyra, have not only fitted the Palmyra area into a map of Palaeolithic Western Asia, but have gone far in producing a skeletal framework for local pre-history. It was no doubt the presence of water which attracted man at this stage—indeed at any stage—but it should be remembered that climatic changes have taken place. Dr Akazawa has found evidence of pollens from vegetation which is not now found in the desert.

Neolithic man knew Ain Efqa, the sulphurous spring, for he left behind him numerous flint flakes and arrowheads in the surrounding area. The same can be said of the site of the Temple of Bel for flints have also been found there, together with pottery fragments from about 2300 to 2200 B.C. attesting to a Bronze Age settlement.

Historical records really begin with the occasional mention of the place, using the apparently pre-Semitic name of Tadmor (by which the town is again known today), in the archives of Kültepe and of Mari where it is given in connection with raids on the village by Sutu nomads. Later, Tiglath-Pileser I of Assyria mentions Tadmor in his chest-thumping campaign history written to celebrate his war against the Aramaeans in 1110 B.C. The following extract shows just what a plague of locusts these campaigning armies were and how smaller, weaker countries had good reason to dread their coming.

Tiglath-Pileser, the legitimate King, King of the World, King of Assyria, King of all the four rims of the earth, the courageous hero who lives guided by the trust-inspiring oracles given him by Ashur and Ninurta, the great gods and his lord, and who thus overthrew all his enemies ... At the command of my lord Ashur I was a conqueror from beyond the Lower Zab River to the Upper Sea (the Mediterranean) which lies towards the West. ... I went to the Lebanon. I cut there timber of cedars for the temple of Anu and Adad, the great gods, my lords, and carried them to Ashur. ... I received tribute from Byblos, Sidon and Avvad, I crossed over in ships belonging to Avvad, from

Avvad which is on the sea shore, to the town Samuri which lies in Amurru a distance of 3 double miles. I killed a narwhal which they call 'sea horse' on high sea. . . .

Twenty-eight times I fought the Ahlamu people and the Aramaeans, once even I crossed the Euphrates twice in one year. I defeated them from Tadmar (Tadmor/Palmyra) which lies in the country of Amurru. . . . I brought their possessions as spoils to my town Ashur.*

The mention of cedarwood as part of his booty is interesting. Because of its strength, marvellous colour and fragrance it was a marketable commodity. Tiglath-Pileser, however, seemed just as pleased with his fishing exploits as with his rapacious conquests.

The Aramaeans remained at Tadmor, despite Tiglath-Pileser having 'defeated them from Tadmar', and were still there in 200 B.C. when the community was large and well enough known to merit a mention in the Old Testament.

The Second Book of Chronicles mentions Tadmor as having been built by Solomon, 'Tadmor in the Desert'. This has long been recognised as a mistake for Tamar which is in the Judean desert. The Chronicler, relying presumably on ancient and now lost texts, felt it necessary to 'correct' the spelling because he knew of Tadmor in the Syrian desert and of its fabulous splendour, but had not heard of Tamar in the Judean desert which enjoyed no claims to fame. By repute, Tadmor was a city worthy of having been built by Solomon, and the Chronicler probably felt that the spelling of Tamar was incorrect. Even though the Biblical quotation does not refer to Tadmor/Palmyra, it is surely indicative that Tadmor/Palmyra was a place of some consequence at that time (approximately 200 B.C.).

During the half millennium before the Christian era, an increasing number of nomads came in from their hostile desert environment and settled in the town. In consequence more than half of the family and personal names known in later, Roman, Palmyra were Arabic in origin, whilst Arab concepts and terms for tribal organisation also made an impact.

'Ownership' of the oasis changed hands with the rise and fall of empires. The Assyrians and the Persians both held it in their turn. With Alexander the Great it came under Macedonian Greek control. Alexander's early death, however, left his empire without a leader of equal stature and it began to break up almost immediately. Eventually, the eastern part of the empire was divided between two of his generals, Seleucus and Ptolemy. Ptolemy took Egypt leaving Seleucus with the satrapy of Babylonia. Seleucus was not one of Alexander's most prominent generals but from the growing chaos he was able to reassemble most of the empire in Asia. This alone marks him as one of the ablest of the Successors, both as a

* J. B. Pritchard: *Ancient Near Eastern Texts.*

military commander and as a statesman. After a setback when he had to flee Babylon, he soon returned, and having defeated Antigonus, he added Syria and Cilicia to his empire.

Thus in approximately 300 B.C. Tadmor fell within the huge Hellenistic Seleucid Empire. Twin capitals were founded, firstly Seleucia on the Tigris in 312 B.C. which effectively replaced Babylon as the entrepôt for trade between east and west. Both Strabo and Pliny mention it, the latter recording that its population reached 600,000! Antioch in the northern Levant was founded twelve years later in 300 B.C. This indicates a growing western bias in Seleucid policy. Psychologically it was also a balance to Seleucia which was remote with greatly overstretched cultural lines of communication.

The twin capital arrangement was to have no immediate effect on Tadmor but it did lay the foundations for her future role.

We know little of what Tadmor looked like at this period. A tell or mound which had grown up on the site of the Temple of Bel was levelled and a temple built upon it. Excavations have suggested that a settlement was to be found along the side of the nearby wadi. The probability is that it was not permanent and that buildings would have been of rather basic construction, most likely of mud brick and with little pretence to architecture and with no fixed luxuries. Trade passing through the town could not have been sufficient to support anything on a grand scale, so the picture is still of a prosperous oasis conveniently placed to afford a short cut across the desert.

The main reason why it is only a trickle of trade is to be found in the animosity between the Seleucid and Ptolemaic Empires. Ptolemy (of Egypt) had extended his boundaries to include Damascus, rather too close to home for the Seleucids. Trade was, therefore, sent on the much longer but, under the circumstances, safer route round the top of the Syrian Desert, a route by which it was certain to end up in Antioch, and not in the hands of Ptolemy in Damascus. In consequence Tadmor was deprived of any benefit from it.

Eventually the Seleucid Empire began to crumble. Not only was it disparate in its character, a curious and uncomfortable union of east and west, but it was also torn for most of its later period by dynastic troubles. To make the situation yet more difficult, the Parthians in the east were gaining strength and pushing their boundaries towards the west, culminating in their conquest of Babylonia. Soon the Seleucid Empire was reduced to Syria alone.

In the west another power, Rome, was flexing her muscles and consuming the Mediterranean world. In 64 B.C. Pompey annexed Antioch, effectively bringing to an end the Seleucid Empire. The city was then made the capital of the new Roman Province of Syria. This new province was restricted to the Levant and its hinterland within the confines of the Fertile Crescent. By establishing Syria as a strong, well organised province Pompey built a dam against the expansion of Parthia. Nonetheless, protracted and fierce wars ensued, Rome sending out expedition after expedition with mixed results. One is reminded particularly of the ambitious Crassus who had spent a lifetime building a platform from which to launch his personal triumph. At the same time as accumulating vast wealth he wheeled and schemed in high politics and places, being in the right place and with the right people at the right time. But despite his distinguished early military career all this political activity deprived him of vital experience in military high command so that when he eventually came face to face with the Parthians he and his army were annihilated.

But what of Tadmor? Suddenly, within a few decades, she found herself between two super-powers yet belonging to neither. War clattered on around them with the Parthians invading Syria and the Romans invading Parthia. The inhabitants of Tadmor must have wondered which of the two would triumph and then descend to devour them. But nothing happened. Miraculously trade between the Roman Province of Syria and Parthia continued to flow—albeit sporadically. At home, Rome was getting richer and more powerful despite long drawn out civil wars, and Parthia was finding the luxury of Hellenised Babylonia very congenial. Parthia began to adopt a veneer of that culture, using Greek administration methods, Greek science, Greek court titles, even getting Greeks to strike their coinage. Both sides still needed the luxuries of life which only trade could supply. Roman society wanted the perfumes of the east, and Parthia needed the imports from the west which were so much a part of the cultural mantle she had opted to wear. Realising this and the uniqueness of their position, the traders and merchants of Tadmor were more than happy to become the middlemen.

Trade continued to flow in the twenty years before Tadmor is again mentioned in ancient texts. The oasis was acting very much as an independent 'state' and began to prosper as never before. This was reflected in the buildings of limestone which increasingly gave the settlement a prosperous appearance. In 44 B.C. the priests of Bel dedicated a sacred image, recorded in an inscription: the fact that it is on a block of limestone indicates that building crafts were reasonably well developed. The inscription has a decorated border, which in turn shows that carvers were at work. Also to this period can be dated the earliest of the tower tombs. The masonry of these strikingly Palmyrene structures was still very irregularly laid, indeed they are referred to today as being of the 'polygonal' type (Fig. 1). These were simple sepulchral towers with little decoration, but they, nonetheless, demonstrate that the craftsmen of Tadmor were able to conceive and undertake work in stone on a monumental scale.

The growing prosperity and wealth of Tadmor were well known. The trading post—it could hardly be called a city—was under no particular domination and

Fig. 1 The Tower Tomb of Kithoth, showing the so-called 'polygonal' construction.

was an easy prey to anyone who was prepared to venture across the desert. In 41 B.C., Mark Antony led a cavalry raid on Tadmor with plunder in mind. But word of his approach had swept ahead of him and when he arrived he found the oasis deserted and empty of anything worth having. The inhabitants had packed up their belongings and sought refuge beyond the Euphrates, taking their wealth with them. Mark Antony came away empty handed.

This incident in Caesar's *Civil War* is important to us on two counts. The fact that the inhabitants withdrew beyond the Euphrates, i.e. into Parthian territory, shows that their instinctive leanings were to the east despite the western, Hellenistic, influences which had been strong throughout the Seleucid era. Even if it had been just a case of moving back in the face of an enemy's advance, they must have been sure of a welcome in Parthian lands, especially when one remembers that they were carrying their entire wealth on their backs. This spiritual link with the east lies at the very base of their culture. It was never to change.

23

It is also illuminating on the condition of Tadmor itself. For the population to be able to pack up all their belongings and wealth at a moment's notice and move a considerable distance shows that, for all the limestone buildings, the population was still not fully settled into an urban life and still clung to many of the ways of the nomad. A fully urbanised and sedentary population would never have been able to pack up and go like this. Housing, therefore, must have been rudimentary—probably mud brick structure of a type which has not changed in thousands of years in the Middle East—and any stone structures would not have been greatly endowed with rich and costly permanent fittings.

It was during Antony's reign that the Parthians were finally expelled, in 38 B.C., from Syria. This was done by his lieutenant, Ventidius, who in 39 B.C. had defeated and killed Labienus, a Roman turncoat and renegade who had led the Parthians into Syria in the first place. But the subjugation of Parthia, about which almost every Roman leader dreamt, was never to come about. The crushing defeat of Crassus must have convinced those who were clear-sighted enough that Parthia could never be crushed. Parthia likewise was forced to admit that expansion into Syria would achieve nothing. As Rostovtzeff has put it, 'both acknowledged the need for peace on the Euphrates, where there were centred commercial interests of vital importance to both. It therefore became essential to compromise and to reach some sort of understanding . . .'* This left Tadmor clearly in the Roman sphere on influence. But being so close to a highly sensitive frontier one must ask how far Rome moved in the initial period towards an actual take-over.

The question of Palmyrene independence is a vexed one. There is no clear and precise date for when Rome brought her under her authority. Certainly Pompey had included the 'city' in his Province of Syria in 64–63 B.C. but at first it seems unlikely that this inclusion was anything more than a claim to the territory. By A.D. 11–12, the Roman Governor of Syria, Creticus Silanus, laid down the territorial boundaries of the Palmyrene state. An arbitrary act unless there was some measure of control to back it up.

Two decades later the name of Germanicus, the Emperor Tiberius's nephew and adopted son, appeared on three local inscriptions. It was at this time that Alexandros of Palmyra, who has already been mentioned, was sent on his embassy to Mesene, 'King' of Spasinu Charax. Statues were put up in the Sanctuary of Bel to Germanicus, Tiberius and Drusus, the Emperor's son. Various entries in the Tariff Law of A.D. 137 also indicate Roman involvement in the administration. As Dr Malcolm A. Colledge has pointed out, 'These references record Roman interference in Palmyra from at least c. A.D. 18.'†

The word interference is important. The Romans were clever at interference

---

* Rostovtzeff: *Caravan Cities.*   † Malcolm A. Colledge: *The Art of Palmyra.*

when their lines of communication were not as strong as they could have wished. There can be no doubt that the Palmyrenes were greedy and Rome probably embarked upon a programme of enticement. It suited her purposes to have Palmyra as a tributary buffer state against the Parthians—but she was wise enough not to take possession of the city. Rather, the evidence points to Rome pouring in funds for building works, affording protection to Palmyrene caravans, and offering administrative help. Certainly during the time of Tiberius we find the first mention of the oasis city in the Roman name of Palmyra rather than the pre-Semitic Tadmor. Also under this emperor's rule there was great building activity. The Temple of Baal Shamin complex was laid out, the old mud brick Temple of Bel was replaced by a splendid stone temple, dedicated in A.D. 32, and the first walls were built.

However, a delicate balance had to be maintained. The stationing of troops at Palmyra had to be organised to give the impression that they were there to help protect and police the trade routes rather than as an invasion force.

Policing trade routes was an important factor for those wishing to attract trade. Undoubtedly some kind of Palmyrene police force gradually evolved. This could have amounted eventually to a small army, growing larger and stronger as its sphere of influence expanded. It is known that the Palmyrene mounted archers were a force with which to reckon in the Roman army. Quite what balance was struck between Roman and local forces is not known, but nominally at least the Roman 'garrison' was there to reinforce the local trade police.

The situation was in many ways similar at Dura-Europos, the city on the Euphrates whose fortunes were so closely linked with those of Palmyra; the only difference being that that city was in the Parthian sphere of influence and there was a Parthian 'garrison' stationed there. Dura-Europos had for long been one of the chain of frontier defences of the Seleucids, but with the Parthians it soon developed into the caravanserai from which merchants went forward to Palmyra. This caravanserai was subject to Parthian interference with Parthian troops and the Dura 'police force' protecting the trade routes up the Euphrates. Thus the desert between the two cities became a neutral no-man's-land with nominally independent buffer states as the forward posts on either side.

Quite what form of agreement there was between Rome and Parthia is not recorded. Not that one would expect there to have been a formal treaty or truce signed between the rival empires, but, rather a tacit understanding of the situation. Again as Rostovtzeff has put it, 'One would rather expect to see on one hand letters from Augustus to his Syrian legate and on the other from the Parthian king to his Mesopotamian satrap, and these might state the terms of some understanding between Rome and Palmyra and between Parthia and Palmyra. Whatever the form of such a correspondence, its effect can hardly be doubted, since it must have enabled Palmyra to become a neutral, semi-independent town, wherein the goods of those two officially hostile powers, Parthia and Rome, might be exchanged.'*

This was just the sort of situation that the Palmyrenes needed. With both Rome and Parthia safeguarding and protecting the city and her boundaries the path lay clear for them to concentrate on trade. Civil organisation had developed to such an extent that the city could provide facilities to justify the taxes and dues she imposed.

Palmyra's history was inextricably tied up with that of external powers, first the Seleucids, then Rome and her rival Parthia. She figured little in the councils of the world. Hers was a sideshow, no doubt full of events but of a kind that did not merit the main stage and the intense, recording lime-light of history. She did not act on her own but was content with the role of middleman in commerce and trade, growing fantastically rich until the setting for the sideshow became one of the most luxurious and elegant in the Province of Syria.

Success was rewarded. The city was proud of those who succeeded and honoured them during their life-times with statues and inscriptions. In fact, it is from honorific inscriptions that we can discover how the caravans were organised. Sometimes these caravans would have been too big for one merchant or even a group of them to finance, so the city contributed to their support. The taxes on trade were clearly regulated and a merchant knew exactly where he stood. The importance of the trade revenues is shown by the fact that 'Treasurers' took precedence even over the City Assembly. The revenues which the Treasurers collected were, in the main, devoted to improving, enlarging and updating temples and their temene and to civic building programmes such as the Agora, main thoroughfares and baths. In the private sector prosperous merchants were laying out fine houses for themselves. The sound of building must have been everywhere, masons, stone carvers, carpenters, artists, all contributing to the clatter and hubbub.

The Emperor Augustus's long reign (31 B.C.–A.D. 14) was marked by his desire for peace in the Middle East. More was achieved then by diplomacy than by the sword. This policy was continued by his immediate successors of the Julio–Claudian House and in consequence Palmyra spun upwards and upwards.

The advent of the Emperor Trajan to the Imperial throne brought changes. In A.D. 106 he annexed Petra and incorporated it into his Province of Arabia with the capital at Bosrah. The trade which had flowed through that fantastic Nabatean capital and empire was now diverted and divided between Egypt and Palmyra. Palmyra thus received a valuable bonus, one which was to put her on the path to becoming the glory of Roman Syria.

---

* Rostovtzeff: *Caravan Cities.*

But Trajan, like Caesar and Pompey, cherished ideas about conquering Parthia. In A.D. 114 he invaded Mesopotamia and having captured Dura-Europos, proceeded down the Tigris, taking the Parthian capital, Ctesiphon, in his stride. The winter of A.D. 115 saw him sunning himself at the mouth of the river. But the Parthians counter-attacked at the base of his lines of communication in Armenia the following year. Simultaneously, southern Mesopotamia rose in revolt. The situation became impossible and was only resolved by Trajan's death in A.D. 117. There was, however, some justification for the invasion. Parthia had always been a menace despite any entente devised under Augustus. In A.D. 110, the Parthian king, Osroes, dethroned the Roman puppet king of Armenia, probably with the intention of annexing that country. This would have greatly endangered the Province of Syria and given Parthia a footing in the eastern Roman world. Had Trajan stopped with the reconquest of Armenia, he would have scored heavily, but the Parthian campaign could not be justified, either tactically or financially, and was as such an act of megalomania.

Trajan's Parthian wars could not have been worse for Palmyra, whose role as middleman was put at risk. If she ceased to be useful as an intermediary, she would become just another provincial trading city in the vast Roman empire. Palmyra would then have been at the mercy of Rome and might have suffered the same fate as Petra.

Mercifully Trajan's successor, Hadrian (A.D. 117–38), reverted to Augustus's policy of peace in the Near and Middle East. Mesopotamia was restored to the Parthians, to be followed shortly afterwards by Dura-Europos. The old balance was restored and the Palmyrenes must have heaved a huge sigh of relief.

In A.D. 129 Hadrian visited Palmyra and the population welcomed him as a second founder of their city. The visit was a lavish and splendid affair. The fact that the whole junket was paid for by a local merchant prince, Malé Agrippa, shows just how rich some Palmyrenes had become. As if this were not enough, in A.D. 139 Malé financed the rebuilding of the Baal Shamin Temple. Both gestures greatly endeared him to the city and established him as one of the most prominent and patriotic of citizens. In return for his tumultuous welcome, Hadrian gave the city the title of *Hadriana*; she was granted 'free' status and a Roman *curator* was installed to look after her finances. During this period, which continued under the majority of Hadrian's successors, Palmyra enjoyed the summer of her fame and fortune. Contact with the west became stronger, indicated by the new habit of adding to their Semitic names Roman family names.

The city was assuming considerable proportions. The civic area we see today, dominated by great stone monuments such as the Sanctuary of Bel, the Monumental Arch and the Colonnade Street, is only a fragment of the total extent of the original city. Beyond, particularly to the south, there extended a huge urban area which was probably built of the time-honoured mud brick (Map 2). Its appearance would have been very much the same as Arab desert architecture before the concrete boxes of today invaded the Middle East: a jumble of irregularly shaped houses with twisting, dusty lanes winding tortuously amid them. Each house had a cluster of ill-lit and ill-ventilated rooms strung round an internal courtyard. Windows were small, to keep out the heat of summer and the bitter cold of winter. This area has had hardly any archaeological examination but the type is familiar.

As far as we know the merchants and wealthy classes lived in the area to the north of the Upper Colonnade Street. Here straight streets divided the blocks of houses, or insulae, and much was built of stone. As with the poorer houses, the majority were built round an open courtyard, but here it was a Hellenistic Greek peristyle (Fig. 2). The family and spacious 'public' rooms were set round this. Again it is a familiar type, recognisable right across the Mediterranean to such far away places as Roman Volubilis in Morocco (where there are very fine examples).

The style of life and degree of comfort depended very much on how well-off one was. For obvious reasons little remains to tell us what living was like for the poorer classes. An artisan quarter has been partly investigated, and from this we have information about the various trades which were followed, but there is little evidence of the living standards and accommodation of this and the unskilled labouring classes. Most of the evidence we have relates to the life of the well-to-do. It was they who could afford fine houses and possibly even finer sepulchres with lavish funerary sculpture.

Externally the houses of the wealthy would have presented blank walls with a doorway to the street (Fig. 3). Inside there was a considerable degree of comfort,

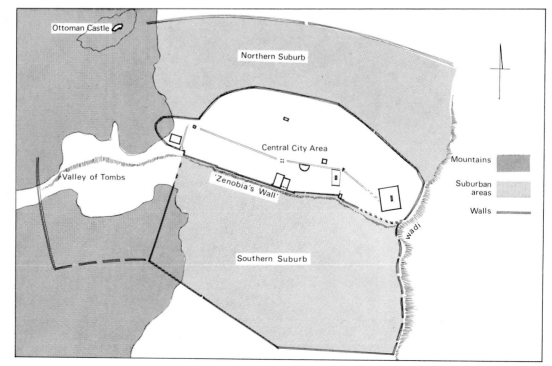

Fig. 2 Reconstruction of the peristyle of a wealthy Palmyrene's house—compare with Fig. 111.

◀ **Map 2** Boundaries of the city at its fullest extent.

Fig. 3 Conjectural reconstruction of a street in the north-eastern quarter of the city.

Fig. 4 Funerary sculpture, a group from the Yarhai Hypogeum which has now been rebuilt in the crypt of the Damascus Museum.

Fig. 5 Carved relief showing the Parthian style of dress.

taste and refinement: frescoes on the walls, mosaics and marble on the floors, with stucco pilasters and other ornament adding a greater feeling of richness. The group of patrician houses which lies to the east of the Sanctuary of Bel (see page 99) is a fine example.

Furniture in the home would have been limited to beds, tables and chairs, and long mattress-covered couches such as those which figure frequently in funerary sculpture (Fig. 4). The sparingness with which furniture was used was offset by the use of rich colour on the walls and ceilings, by the pottery and glass used, and above all by the use of fabrics and rugs.

Pottery has been found in great quantities. Lamps, jugs, jars, bowls, amphorae were imported during the Hellenistic period from both east and west. Local pottery was, however, in production by 100 B.C. and this had so developed by the time the Romans arrived that the import of pottery became unnecessary. There is nothing particularly special or distinctive about Palmyrene pottery; in the main it followed the Hellenistic types common enough in the Middle East. Many of the funerary sculptures show vessels, cups and containers, all richly decorated. However not one such cup has ever been found, and it is probable that the lavish ware shown in the reliefs depicts metal cups, bowls and amphorae, goods which would have long ago disappeared—if not into the melting pot of history, into the melting pot of some metal-hungry Arab. No metal vessels have, however, ever been found in an undisturbed burial assemblage.

Glass was imported from the coastal regions of Syria where there were famous manufactures. It was, however, made eventually in Palmyra, as lumps of crude

30

glass found in the artisans' quarter have shown, but it is unlikely that this locally produced ware would ever have graced a wealthy table or been thought good enough to find a place in a tomb.

The Palmyrenes were quite prepared to spend a lot on dress—and on jewellery. Sculpture shows the styles which prevailed but obviously not the fabrics which were used. Fortunately three of the tower tombs, Iamliku, Elahbel and No. 46, have yielded a considerable number of fragments which give a good idea of the materials used and their decoration. It is not safe to rely on the decoration shown in sculpture because many of the actual designs were so complex and elaborate that the sculptures had to fall back on a simplified repertoire of designs.

Linen was widely used to make the tunic which was so popular (Fig. 5) and it was always used in its natural colour. Even the cloak which was worn over the tunic was sometimes made of linen. It is quite possible that there were winter and summer weight garments; the linen cloak in summer would have been cool whilst the same article in wool would have been extremely warm in the bitterly cold winters in the Syrian Desert. The tunic frequently had an embroidered collar and cuffs, whilst the cloak could have decorated borders on the two short sides with the possible addition of a fringe.

Cotton was rare, but wool was widely used both for garments and for decorative embroidery. It was with wool that colour was introduced in a dramatic range of warm, vivid tones. The favourites were reds and dark blues, browns and purples sometimes embellished with gold. Wool was also used to make the tunic, and the Parthian style trouser leggings (Fig. 5), and the Persian style riding coats with their practical flared bottoms, seems always to have been fashioned in wool. Mattress covers were also of wool. The decoration relied markedly upon stripes and bands of colour containing stylised motifs. Floral patterns and the repeating geometric designs so conspicuous in their architectural decoration were used with great panache. Fabrics were closely woven giving depth to the colours.

It is with silk that we really sense the lavishness with which the Palmyrenes dressed themselves and with which they may also have furnished their houses. Only tiny fragments have survived, so it is not possible to tell which garments were made of this precious material. It was imported from the east, even though there is no textual evidence for this, the patterns being quite unlike anything to be found in the Mediterranean at that time, or in the Middle East. Intertwining and repetitive designs were woven in glowing colours along with bands of stylised flowers and nightmarish animals clawing their way through the silken undergrowth.

There was no great difference between male and female fashions, only that women became, as time went on, almost laden down with jewellery (men hardly wore any at all) and they added a veil to their outfit. The use of the veil before Islam is a fascinating subject. It is wrong to suppose that it was Koranic in origin,

31

even in Arabia. The late Père Roland de Vaux referring to a trio of veiled women (Fig. 6) on a beam in the Temple of Bel, brought together some impelling evidence on the subject.*

The pre-Islamic poet of the second century, Al Mufaddal bin Muhammad, in his poem *Mufaddaliyat* mentions veiling of women. The Latin commentator Tertullian in *De virginibus velandis* (a text which can be dated to approximately the same period as the beam in the Temple of Bel) advises Christian women to follow Arabian women who veil completely in public, leaving only a slit for one eye. This is very much the type of arrangement which is shown in the Bel relief, which in all probability represents Palmyrene women in their outdoor dress. The origin probably lies in Assyrian law, in fact, from a Middle Assyrian legal code enacted by Tiglath–Pileser I (the same who smote the Aramaeans) in the twelfth century B.C., though the laws contained in the Code may go back to the fifteenth century. This Code was found at Ashur by a German archaeological excavation between 1903 and 1914. It was one of a series of important Mesopotamian legal codes like that of Hammurabi who ruled Amorite Babylon between 1792 and 1759 B.C., and that of Lipit-Ishtar who was the fifth ruler of the first dynasty of Isin and who ruled during the twentieth century B.C. (1934–1924 B.C.).

The Ashur Code states that 'neither wives of seignors nor widows who go out on the street may have their heads uncovered. The daughters of a seignor whether it is with a shawl or a robe or a mantle must veil themselves. . . . A concubine who goes out on the street with her mistress must veil herself. A sacred prostitute whom a man married must veil herself on the street, but one whom a man did not marry must have her head uncovered on the street; she must not veil herself. A harlot must not veil herself; her head must be uncovered; he who has seen a harlot veiled must arrest her, produce witnesses and bring her to the palace tribunal; they shall not take her jewellery away, but the one who arrested her may take her clothing; . . . they shall flog her fifty times with staves and pour pitch on her head. However if a seignor has seen a harlot veiled and has let her go without bringing her to the palace tribunal, they shall flog the seignor fifty times with staves; his prosecutor shall take his clothing; they shall pierce his ears, thread them with a cord and tie it at the back of his head, and he shall do the work of the King for one full month. Female slaves shall not veil themselves.

'If a seignor wishes to veil his concubine, he shall have five or six of his neighbours present and shall veil her in their presence and say "she is my wife" and so she becomes his wife. A concubine who was not veiled in the presence of the men, whose husband did not say "she is my wife" is not a wife; she is still a concubine. . . .'†

From this it is clear that, as Père de Vaux points out, free women and daughters

---

* *Revue Biblique*, 1935.　　　　　　† *Ancient Near Eastern Texts*, ed. by J. B. Pritchard.

Fig. 6 Veiled women, part of a relief from one of the beams of the Temple of Bel.

Fig. 7 Sepulchral portrait known as 'The Beauty of Palmyra'.

of free men, together with servants attending a woman outdoors, and legitimately married slaves, had to wear a veil when they went out. Unmarried slaves, prostitutes and servants on their own were not allowed to veil themselves. 'The interpretation of the Code is clear, a wife belongs to her husband, the virgin to her father, and so they must be recognised as such, and their charms must not be shown to everyone.' This ensured that a respectable woman would be free from the abuse which might otherwise be meted out to a courtesan or slave. The veil therefore becomes a way of distinguishing between classes. The same motive can be attributed to the Koranic injunction, with the Prophet thus confirming a social rule but thereby giving the veil a religious aura. 'It will be easier that they should be recognised from the slave girl and servant and should not therefore be offended.'*

Palmyrene women felt no such inhibitions about jewellery. As time went on they decked themselves with rings, necklaces, tiaras and collars (Fig. 7). The number of

* *Koran, 'Soura' 33:59.*

33

items increased until eventually their chests became wholly covered by them, often with pendants off necklaces and amulets. Brooches were worn, particularly on the left shoulder as a pin to hold the cloak in place. Unfortunately very little jewellery has been discovered and we have to rely on sculpture and paintings to find out what was worn.

Silver, bronze and gold were set with a variety of stones and glass paste. Early pieces occasionally employed glazed faience and cornelian, schist and polished limestone. Much of the jewellery was made in Palmyra as attested by an inscription of A.D. 258 set up by the 'Corporation of gold and silversmiths'. However, the style and type of work shows such a wide variety of influences and characters that probably a considerable amount was also imported.

It is not known with any certainty what rich women did with their time: perhaps this is a perennial question. On the other hand, men of the leisured classes would have led anything but leisured lives. For the majority the business of trade and its attendant services such as banking would have kept them busy. For those who had risen from the 'purple of commerce' there were civic, religious and sometimes Imperial affairs to attend to.

The Assembly was first mentioned in a Roman text dated A.D. 24/25, along with the Treasurers. The Senate is thought to have been established during the reign of Nero (A.D. 54–68) although it is first mentioned in A.D. 74. At this time, too, the four leading tribes with sectional municipal authority first appear. The Treasurers took precedence over the Assembly because it was they who collected the revenues. The presence of a Roman *curator* still further complicates the question of how Palmyra was governed, and by whom. There can be little doubt that Rome continued to strengthen her position, but this was tactfully done. Local affairs were left in local hands so that Rome did not appear to be a conquering force, but she kept a grip on the city's political dealings abroad. Rome never made the mistake of dipping her hands into the revenues she oversaw; her dues were collected by declared and specified taxes.

The people of Palmyra would have been subjected all the time to the highly efficient Roman propoganda machine which emphasised the huge benefits derived from 'association' with Rome and which minimised the fact that there was precious little in the way of an option. For much of the 'historical' period of Palmyra, the people were more intent on pursuing the path of commercial prosperity than an enemy for a few acres of useless land.

The conduct of trade, for which the Palmyrenes had a natural inclination and a practical genius, was balanced by a passionate spiritual belief in their gods. More the pity then that we know so little about their pantheon and its development, and the rituals which attended it. There is no ancient text which gives a clear, concise picture, and scholars have had to fit the jig-saw together with rather too many pieces missing. It is known that they had a great many gods, nearly all of them imported, but there were two main triads.

The great god Bel, to whom the largest and most splendid sanctuary was dedicated, was Babylonian in origin. He had two companions who shared his temple, and who were very ancient and probably Palmyrene in origin, Iarhibol and Aglibol. The other triad consisted of the Phoenician Baal Shamin who shared his beautiful sanctuary with Aglibol again and another local, Malakbel.

Behind these two dominant triads were ranged a host of other deities, Babylonian Nebo, Nergal and Nanai, Canaanite Belhammon, Sadrafa and Elqonera, and Babylonian Atargatis and Ishtar. From the Arabs who had come and settled in ancient Tadmor came Samas and the great goddess Allat, so deeply revered by the Arab Nabateans of Petra. When one remembers that the Prophet Mohammed overthrew 360 different tribal idols in the temple when he entered Mecca in triumph, one can see that pre-Moslem Arab religions had an extensive pantheon consisting mostly of tribal and local deities. How many of these came and settled in Palmyra is debatable; we can only record names which appear in inscriptions.

Judging by the scale of the Bel and Baal Shamin sanctuaries it is reasonable to suggest that these gods and their companion deities were held to be the most important. For the relevant importance of the other gods, the only guide is the comparative number of inscriptions relating to each. The antiquity of the deity does not seem to have mattered. Allat and Nebo ranked close seconds to Bel and Baal Shamin, for they both had sanctuaries of their own (see pages 181 and 134) and are frequently mentioned.

Apart from the 'great goddess Allat' and Babylonian Ishtar, women do not seem to have featured much in the pantheon. As with Mesopotamia and Arabia, Palmyra was very much a male orientated world—both spiritually and temporally. This is not to say that outstanding women like Allat could not succeed in penetrating the male domain of power, as we soon shall see.

We can only conjecture at what 'departments' of life and death each was responsible for. Sepulchral evidence from Palmyra tends to equate Allat with Athena, helmeted and with one hand holding a spear and the other resting on a shield. The Arab historian, Ibn al Kelbi, recounts her worship in Arabia so she must have arrived in Tadmor with the settling bedouin. Bel was the 'Lord' or 'Master' and the Greeks correlated him with Zeus. By having as his companions Iarhibol and Aglibol, the sun and moon gods respectively, he was worshipped as a 'cosmic god' responsible for the destinies of men and matters which the ancients, particularly the Mesopotamians, believed were regulated by the stars. This would account for the astrological ceiling in the north adyton of the Temple of Bel (see page 122).

As though to confuse the issue, the Greeks also equated Baal Shamin with Zeus, for he was 'Lord of the Heavens'. He is, however, frequently portrayed in sculpture as a huge eagle with outspread wings, covering the moon, sun and stars. When he decided to take on human form he varied his attire, sometimes in armour, sometimes in the local dress. He had as his symbols or attributes thunderbolts and ears of corn.

Like the Ephesians, the Palmyrenes seem to have been concerned that no god should feel neglected and so they also had their unnamed deity who is variously called 'Lord of the World', 'Him whose Name is blessed for ever' and 'The Nameless God'. Dr Colledge considers that he is identical with Baal Shamin because these epithets were also given to him, whilst the nameless god also has Aglibol and Malakbel as associates.

Nebo was sometimes paired with Apollo (e.g. the second or third century statue of Apollo found in the Nebo Sanctuary), who looked after music, archery, prophecy, medicine and had the care of flocks and herds. He was often associated with the higher developments of civilisation, approving codes of law, inculcating high moral and religious principles, and philosophy. Nergal was equated with Hercules who was a hero, not a god. Nonetheless, a powerful cult grew up about Hercules's name and he was occasionally worshipped for his hardiness, valour in the service of mankind, and for his supposed ability to avert evil of all kinds. His cult was particularly popular with merchants, no doubt because of the long and successful journeys involved in his Labours.

These gods gaze at us today from sculptures which, as an art form, are unmistakably Palmyrene. Although there was much imported sculpture, particularly of bronze—see the Tariff (page 17)—from the Hellenistic west, little remains. In any case its style would have been typical of late Roman work and be unrelated to the religious and funerary sculpture which is so distinctive of Palmyra. This must have applied to a great quantity of public statuary in Palmyra. That so much of it has disappeared is due to its having been melted down for utilitarian purposes during the Dark Ages (and in the West as much as in the East). Also, being very prominent, it would have been a prime target for the iconoclastic fury evoked by the famous decree of Caliph Yazid II (A.D. 720–24) which ordered the destruction of all human images and pictures in Moslem lands. Yazid was an Ummayyad whose 'capital' was at Damascus, to which Palmyra was uncomfortably close. Certainly Dr Halifax, writing in 1691, reported that the sculptures in the tower tombs were 'miserably defaced and broken', and although this does not apply to all sculptures known today, it is true of a vast number.

If Palmyra was influenced by Rome politically she was as much influenced by Parthia culturally. She was western oriental in her beginning and remained so until the end. Despite the Hellenistic sculptural and painting techniques she adopted and the Graeco–Roman motifs she employed, her art remains an expres-

Fig. 8 Relief on one of the beams of the Temple of Bel showing Palmyrene deities.

sion of the Parthian artistic language. At first it appears very much as a naïve handling of the classical formal repertoire. This was a means to an end, and the naïvety is in reality a reduction of realism to a limited and easily recognisable number of formulae. These formulae enabled the artist to achieve an unworldliness and timelessness in his portrayal of a subject, be it a religious relief or a portrait of a merchant. Hellenistic art strove to achieve an ideal of beauty or a display of realism. By denying realism and concentrating on spiritual character Parthian art tended towards the abstract. Reality was not abandoned however, for Palmyrene iconographic art never became wholly abstract. To demonstrate this there is a fascinating series of portrait sculptures in the Palmyra Museum of the family of Zabida, son of Ogaili (A.D.112), which all show a quite remarkable family likeness. Portraiture in the western world emerged in the early Hellenistic period with some almost breath-taking bronzes but the preoccupation with the 'ideal' still permeated the works.

Turning first to groups, it will be noted that each figure is placed separately with hardly any overlapping at all, with everyone standing or sitting on the same level (Fig. 8). Also, the face, if not the whole body, is turned full to the spectator, the pose is stiff, even rigid, and there is an unearthly calm about them (Fig. 4). There are no representations of violent action or emotion. This way of showing a banquet, procession or whatever was repeated continuously; it was the formula.

37

The frontal positioning of characters in so four-square a way was also a formula. One can see that this practice would have accorded with their philosophy, for a frontal representation brought one into direct face-to-face contact with the character portrayed. Present day phrases express the same meaning: if you want to impress something on someone, the most effective way to do it is to come 'face-to-face' with them, you 'confront' them.

This is the real nub of Palmyrene and Parthian art, it is direct. By reducing the subject to a series of formulae, then freezing them into a scheme of arrangement, the complicating and confusing issue of aesthetics is avoided. A veiled woman is represented by a curling, idiomatic, sweep of lines almost to the point of abstraction, for example the carving on the beam from the Temple of Bel. The folds of drapery are simplified and realism is almost obliterated. Likewise, in other portrait sculptures (Fig. 9), hair is represented in two or three ways only, jewellery is chunky and concerned with form rather than with precise detail, gesture is limited to a few standard poses. Eyes are enlarged and predominantly almond shaped, the whole modelling of a face is based on a stereotype within which individuality and personality are also expressed.

All these attributes are exemplified in the so-called 'Beauty of Palmyra' from the early third century (Fig. 7): the right arm bent across the body, the left hand held up grasping lightly the edge of the veil as if she were about to cover her face. The ropes of jewellery on her chest are there in abundance, the brooch to hold the cloak together is there just below her left shoulder, the veil draped rather stiffly over the top of her richly bejewelled hair-do, the almond eyes, the straight Asiatic nose and even more Asiatic mouth. She faces one with an unearthly air despite her very earthly finery, composed, timeless, transfixed, spiritual. Yet—there is an earthy sensuality, a dominant personality combined with a sense of belonging and awareness of social position, all of which give her character. Without doubt the wife of a very rich man but one not without the frailty of human desires and designs.

The same formula can be seen in the portrait of an elderly lady (Fig. 10), yet here is a markedly different personality; her bland, withdrawn, almost bemused expression hints at sad, uncomprehending resignation. Not so with Aqmat, daughter of Hagago (Fig. 11), from the late second century, a bossy looking matron who grips her veil with aggressive determination. She is not withdrawn, rather she gives the impression of relishing the cut and thrust of her times. Iarhibola, from the third century (Fig. 12), is typical of a man, so too are the recumbent figures from the Yarhai Hypogeum (Fig. 4—see page 198), who display all the accepted formulae whilst exuding individual personality. All these faces are of people who are clearly distinguishable, yet they are all typically Palmyrene.

Fig. 9 Sepulchral portrait illustrating one of the sculptural conventions for depicting hair.

Fig. 10 Sepulchral portrait of an unknown elderly lady.

Fig. 12 Sepulchral portrait of Iarhibola whose priestly hat is shown, draped with the curtain of death, over his right shoulder.

Fig. 11 Sepulchral portrait of Aqmat, daughter of Hagago.

PALMYRA

Architecture as an expression of the art of Palmyra is dealt with in a later chapter. But before leaving the world of sculpture we must say something about a feature which we have not so far looked at and which appears in a small group of works in the Museum. This is the use of a curtain, sometimes entirely on its own, sometimes hung behind (Fig. 13), and, rarely, in front of a person. Frequently a palm frond appears on either side at the top of the curtain. What does this mean? There is no certain answer, but it is always associated with funerary art, indeed it appears countless times on headstones as well as on funerary reliefs. There are a number of possible answers. It could be taken as the division between life and death, the veiled mystery of the afterlife. In Hellenistic art it is frequently used to denote the interior of a house; thus in funerary art it could be read as indicating the deceased's eternal home. There is also the possibility that it represents the veil behind which the deities are enthroned. The Palmyrenes were Semitic and although certainly not Hebrew there is a common base to their cultures. Could this, then, be an allusion to the Veil of the Temple transmuted at some early stage into the Aramaean culture? The deities of Palmyra, when they travelled, were carried in curtained palanquins on camels. The deity would not have been seen, in fact Bel and his companions may never have left the north adyton of the temple, seen only by the priests, dummies enshrined in the south adyton being those which were ritually paraded at religious festivals.

Palmyrene painting was, as one might expect, bright and colourful. Sculpture, both reliefs and portraits, as well as architectural embellishments, was richly coloured also. The painting of tomb (particularly hypogea) interiors with figurative and architectural designs was extensively practised. There are some fine examples extant, e.g. the Tomb of the Three Brothers (Fig. 14 and see page 205), a work of unrivalled magnificence which dates from A.D. 160–191. The practice of using paintings on a plaster base can be dated back with certainty to A.D. 40, e.g. Kithoth's Tower Tomb (see page 193). It was often used in association with stone embellishments; an interior might have sculpture, both figurative and architectural, further architectural details in stucco and fresco surfaces. The work differs markedly from Roman productions although elements of the classical repertoire are used. It is akin to similar work at Dura-Europos and recalls very strongly the character of Palmyrene sculpture and decorative detail. The style is fully in the mainstream of Palmyrene art. Architectural painting on ceilings, vaults and walls repeats many of the complicated geometric designs so beloved of the Palmyrenes (Fig. 14). In its rich colouring it gives us an idea of how striking many of the buildings must have looked with their architectural details picked out in strong colours. The grandeur of buildings became truly spectacular.

And indeed, by the second century A.D. Palmyra was assuming an air of spectacular grandeur. Like so many cities she flowered under Hadrian's liberal

Fig. 13 A grave stone showing a 'curtain of death' draped behind the deceased.

Fig. 14 Frescoes on the barrel vault and walls of the Three Brothers Hypogeum.

rule. All this feverish activity kept the coins pouring happily into the Treasury thus allowing the city to afford its civic spending spree on public architecture. The Hellenistic style which had burst upon Tadmor/Palmyra with the Temple of Bel was now taken up and developed in a very distinctive way. Rich decoration was lavished on original and inventive shapes and forms. To some the opulence of the architecture is excessive, as though the Palmyrenes had believed in Oscar Wilde's dictum 'Nothing succeeds like excess'. For them there is indeed a certain lack of moderation in the ebullience with which carving was used and in the way architecture was made to bend into almost acrobatic contortions. But the designers had a sense of rightness by which they were able to leave enough flat, smooth face of stone for the enrichment to make its fullest impact.

Fig. 15 The Temple of Baal Shamin from the east courtyard.

It was during the Antonine dynasty that the Temenos of the Temple of Bel was completed, with its vast colonnades and huge Propylaea. Baal Shamin got a smart, crisp new temple and another colonnaded courtyard to his sanctuary (Fig. 15). The tall, distinctive tower tombs gave way to funerary temples with richly architectural interiors and pillared porticos, and glowingly coloured hypogea. The spacious colonnaded Agora was built (Fig. 16) with the so-called Tariff Court next door (Fig. 92) as an integral part of the structure. The Tariff Court was fronted on the south side with an entrance portico of massive dimensions. The theatre,

42

Fig. 16 Aerial view of the Agora.

backing onto the main street, was built in the Roman tradition, its *scaenae frons* almost rivalling that at Bosrah in its magnificence. Behind, the main thoroughfare underwent a traumatic change, emerging as the grandiose Colonnade Street we see today (Fig. 100).

Of course it was all thoroughly nouveau riche and ostentatious but it was a marvellous, self-confident expression of self-made prosperity, unfettered by neuroses about expense or propriety. Palmyra had arrived. In just over a century she had come from being an out-of-the-way village in the back of beyond to a metropolis whose fame, wealth and glamour were attracting immigrants from all over the world, including the history and culture-steeped lands of Egypt and Greece.

43

PALMYRA

Fearful of losing her so-called 'neutral' status, Palmyra did not become too deeply involved in the conquest of northern Mesopotamia by Marcus Aurelius's co-Emperor, Lucius Verus. This campaign led to the capture of Dura-Europos in A.D. 165 and the establishment there of a Roman garrison in place of the Parthian. A new unit in the Roman army, the twentieth cohort, was posted there—a cohort made up of Palmyrene soldiers. How Parthia felt about this conquest we do not know, but they cannot have been too pleased to learn that a unit made up of Palmyrenes was part of the force which now held their land captive. It was like a betrayal. One can believe that Palmyra tried hard to explain the situation but in the long term it was to have restricting results.

The civil disorders which followed the end of the Antonine dynasty and which saw the Severi rise to power, did not greatly affect Palmyrene trade. Under Septimius Severus, the age of opulence continued but the arrival of the new dynasty brought a period of great change and innovation into the affairs of the city. The Province of Syria was divided, with Palmyra finding itself in the 'Phoenician' half. Control by the Roman garrison posted just outside the city was tightened.

Commemorative inscriptions in the past had mentioned cities far afield, deep into Parthian territory. Now, rather suddenly, there is no mention of Spasinu Charax or Mesene. Can one read into this that Parthia was restricting Palmyrene dealings to Babylonia alone? There were also cracks beginning to show in security along the routes across the desert. After Septimius Severus, campaigns against Parthia became the stock-in-trade of Roman emperors, and her armies were fully committed to campaign duties. This forced the Palmyrenes to strengthen their own police force to deal with the deteriorating situation.

Despite this, building flourished in the city; the Colonnade Street was pushed in the direction of the Temple of Bel and house building for the wealthy continued apace including some lavish and opulent houses east of the Bel Sanctuary.

With the death of Severus Alexander in A.D. 235, the centre of power crumbled and control of the far flung empire began to disintegrate. Rome was for forty years a jungle of intrigue, blood and uncertainty, as one short-lived emperor followed another. The rule of law and order in the empire was a shadow and pretence. The emperor's death brought home to the Palmyrenes the seriousness of the situation. He had made gallant efforts to restore law and order with his armies fully committed on several fronts. Palmyra could, therefore, expect little military help from Rome and this led to the strengthening of the local army in order to effect some kind of security along the trade routes. She could not now look to Parthia, for that imperial star had set and a new force had arisen in the east, the Persian Sassanians. Thrown back on her own resources, Palmyra had to cope. The fact that the central Roman authority was unable to control events meant that the Palmyrenes had to manage their own political and administrative affairs as well.

The city suddenly became more autonomous than she had ever been, and this led inevitably to local factions out of which one of the four principal tribal families, the Julii Aurelii Septimii, steadily rose to power. They were to play the leading part in the final chapter of classical Palmyra before her ignominious fall and eclipse.

Edessa and Nisibis, two petty states in the north of the Fertile Crescent, revolted, an event which started the gradual move of trade routes away from Palmyra. The Sassanians drove westwards round the Fertile Crescent and conquered nearly all Syria, arriving at the gates of Antioch. The Emperor Valerian (A.D. 253–60) campaigned against them with disaster after disaster culminating in his capture at Edessa in A.D. 260. His fate thereafter is unknown. His son, Gallienus, who had been co-Augustus with him, now had to deal with the uprisings which were occurring all over the empire.

Meanwhile, back in Palmyra, the Julii Aurelii Septimii had become so powerful that their leader, Septimius Odainat, was un-crowned King of Palmyra. Behind him he had a strong army. At about the same time that Valerian was captured, Septimius Odainat emerged as Governor of Phoenician Syria. He immediately declared war on the Persians and for eight years he achieved success upon success, pushing the Sassanians back. In A.D. 260 he crushingly defeated Sapur, the Sassanian monarch. Gallienus rewarded his loyalty with the title *Restitutor totius Orientis—Corrector of all the East*—an honour previously borne by the emperors alone. Odainat, however, went a stage further. Having smashed the Persian King, he claimed the Persian style and title 'King of Kings'. Rome did nothing about this display of autonomy; she was much too preoccupied elsewhere and in any case Palmyra had shown her loyalty in a very practical way when so many others had turned against the Eternal City. Odainat, however, meant to be regarded as King, and set up his court to which he attracted men of distinction and achievement. Perhaps to make sure of his conquest he campaigned twice in Sassanian Mesopotamia but was eventually murdered in A.D. 267, it was said at the instigation of his wife.

He was succeeded by his second son, Wahballat (the first son by a previous marriage had mysteriously died at the same time as Odainat was murdered). Wahballat was a minor so his mother, Bat Zabbai, better known to history as Queen Zenobia, acted as regent. The seizure of total power by this ambitious woman was taken by Rome as a danger signal. The Emperor Gallienus sent Haraclianus against her but, with the army that had smashed Sapur and the Sassanians, she proceeded to defeat the Roman general. Had she stopped there things might have been all right, but she went on to seize the whole of the Province of Syria. She then besieged and devastated Bosrah, the capital city of the Province of Arabia. In A.D. 269, to the utter amazement of the world, she invaded Egypt. In a year she had conquered it, so that by A.D. 270 she was able to turn her attentions

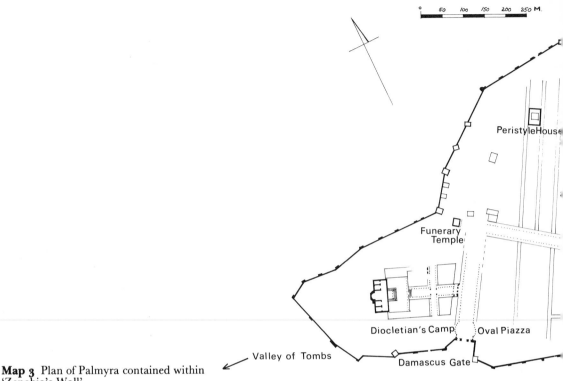

0   50   100   150   200   250 M.

PeristyleHouse

Funerary
Temple

Diocletian's Camp   Oval Piazza

Valley of Tombs

Damascus Gate

Map 3 Plan of Palmyra contained within
'Zenobia's Wall'.

to Asia Minor. No one before had challenged the Empire in such a way and with
such success.

But Rome was now in the hands of a hardened cavalry officer, Aurelian, who
was beginning to pull the empire together again. His initial tactic was to acquiesce
in Queen Zenobia and grant her son, Wahballat, all the titles and honours his
father had enjoyed. It is significant that he 'granted' these titles, thereby restating
his Roman authority and claim over Palmyra.

Zenobia's ambition would not tolerate this—she was queen of an independent,
seemingly all-powerful and autonomous state. In her eyes, therefore, she, or at
least her son for whom she was regent, stood on a level footing with the Roman
Emperor. In A.D. 271 she affirmed as much by proclaiming her son 'Augustus'.
This was too much for Aurelian.

The general Probus was sent to Egypt whilst Aurelian himself took command of
the reconquest of Asia Minor. This he achieved without much difficulty. He was
soon at the gates of Antioch and forced Zenobia's general, Zabdas, to retreat to
Emesa (present day Homs). There Aurelian inflicted another defeat on him
leaving the road open to Palmyra.

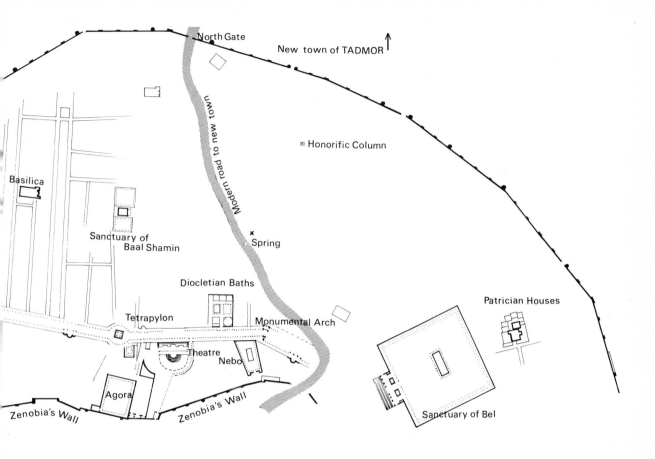

It was quite impossible for the depleted Palmyrene army to defend the city. It is believed that the inner wall which cuts the original city in two (Map 3) was hurriedly raised so that at least the civic quarter could be defended. This today is called 'Zenobia's Wall' (see page 211).

Zenobia, in a final, desperate bid for independence, slipped through the siege lines and headed for the Euphrates and the Sassanians from whom she intended to beg help. After the defeats her husband had inflicted upon them it is debatable how far Sapur would have been willing to come to her aid. If she succeeded it would have been at a considerable price: whichever way it went, a defeat at the hands of Aurelian and his Roman legions or a highly priced alliance with Sapur, the independence of Palmyra was lost. The question never arose because she was captured whilst crossing the river and was carried back to Aurelian's camp. Later, in August A.D. 272, Palmyra capitulated.

Possibly because Aurelian already had enough on his plate, or perhaps because he admired the courage and beauty of the defeated queen, he spared her life and the city. Nonetheless he deprived the Palmyrenes of any chance of new leadership by putting to death a selection of the leading citizens, including Cassius Longinus.

Fig. 17 Coin bearing the image of
Queen Zenobia.

Leaving only as strong a garrison as was necessary he led Zenobia off back to
Rome.

Sources conflict as to what happened to her after this. Some say she died on the
journey, others that she was slaughtered with Longinus and the others. The most
generally accepted story relates that she figured in Aurelian's triumph in Rome
and was then given a pension and a villa at Tivoli—and probably a strong guard.
Her obscure end must have irked her but her city was destined to have no such
quiet swan song.

In A.D. 273, within months of Aurelian's departure, the city rose and slaughtered the garrison. The reason for this may be that the Roman forces had laid on
the conquerors' act, abusing the Palmyrenes until outrage became unbearable. In
any event, Aurelian hurried back, entered the city unopposed and then let his
troops go on the rampage, looting, killing, burning, destroying. The glory that had
been Palmyra was finished.

It is easy to dismiss the tragic end of Palmyra as the work of a megalomaniac
woman whose ambition got the better of her. But there was more to Zenobia than
just ambition. Coins that bear her image (Fig. 17) give us some idea of her looks
and she was famous for her beauty. She was also reputedly highly intelligent. One
could argue that her contest with Rome was the exact opposite of an intelligent act.
Yet she was able to attract to her Court some of the best minds in the Hellenistic
world including Cassius Longinus, the rhetorician and philosopher. He became
her principal adviser, and surely there must have been a meeting of kindred spirits
and minds or he would not have stayed. 'On the Sublime', a work of the first
importance in which the quality of literary thought is put under a critical micro-
scope and illumined with unprecedented clarity and sophistication, is often attributed to him but this work was probably written in the first century A.D. and so
Zenobia's Longinus was almost certainly not the author.

Her virtue was also highly praised but—rather as with Elizabeth I of England—it was probably moral or sexual virtue which is implied. Perhaps her passion for living gave vent to itself in battles of the mind rather than of the bed, and in ruthless, overvaulting ambition rather than in the pursuit of physical satisfaction. The fact that she was tough to the point of savagery on the one hand and meek yet thoughtful—and possibly physically cold—on the other makes her one of the most fascinating characters to stride across the sandy pages of the Ancient Middle East. Under such stimulus and leadership one can imagine how exciting and adventurous it was to live amid the golden pillars and green palms of Palmyra in her heyday.

Palmyra was never able to revive herself. The actual damage which Aurelian's army managed to do was, in all probability, quite slight—there was certainly not a wholesale destruction of the city. But the shock to the system was more than it could take. The arts and certain aspects of her national life ceased abruptly. There was no further architectural development—in fact little more architecture at all. Also, the trade routes further north were beginning to gather popularity and the pendulum of prosperity was swinging away from Palmyra.

It was its strategic importance as a forward base on the eastern frontiers that prevented the city from returning to the desert. In about A.D. 300 the Emperor Diocletian (A.D. 284–305) repaired the western part of the town and created the last major architectural complex in the place, a formidable military camp (see page 184). Life would have continued as in any provincial town in the weakening empire. The city shrank and became centred in the civic area behind the 'Zenobia' wall.

Despite the persecutions of Diocletian, Christianity was gaining strength in the town for in A.D. 325 the Bishop of Palmyra, Marinos, participated in the Council of Nicaea. The restoration work on the Colonnade Street in the years following A.D. 327 gave a glimmer of hope that things might improve. Two basilicas were built which were modest enough structures in a city so recently given to grandeur. Probably much of the material for their building was looted from other, decaying structures. Early in the fifth century the Temples of Bel and of Baal Shamin were turned into churches.

One has a picture of the town as rather a neglected place with a vast, evacuated and crumbling suburb to the south. Amid the pillars the township picked a living, acting as a frontier post against perils beyond the Euphrates. It must have felt very isolated, no longer enjoying the material security of a special place in the Roman Empire. The bond which gave it meaning within the context of the 'known' world was Christianity. The city was part of a Brotherhood, not part of a Province. The Emperor in Constantinople was the ruler, but he was remote and service to him was undertaken as service to Christianity.

The Emperor Justinian (A.D. 527–65) ordered the renovation of all the churches and fortifications in Palmyra. This indicates that it was still important enough to figure in imperial concerns. But with the eventual collapse of the Western Roman Empire and all it had stood for, there came the final blow to classical Palmyra, Islam.

The Prophet Mohammed succeeded in consolidating a religious state in Arabia before he died in A.D. 632, but he left no nominated successor or any clear indication as to how the successors were to be chosen. There followed the First or Orthodox Caliphs who had been his immediate companions—a natural and reasonable solution. Each was nominated and elected at Medina, but a struggle soon developed between those who regarded Ali and his descendants as the only rightful contenders for the Caliphate, a faction known as the Shiites, and those who held that the Caliphate was an elected position open to all members of the Prophet's tribe, the Kuraish. This latter faction was known as Sunnites.

Despite the mounting friction, the Orthodox Caliphs saw the boundaries of Islam pushed far beyond the peninsula confines of Arabia. All Lower Egypt, Cyrenaica and Tripolitania in North Africa were converted, as well as Syria, Mesopotamia and Iran. In many areas the population at all levels welcomed the new force and it was not really a case of conquest. Nonetheless, the armies of Islam seemed to be everywhere. Palmyra, however, resisted.

Khalid ibn al Walid, one of the first Caliph's most outstanding generals, had been fighting a campaign in Mesopotamia when he was recalled to support Abu Obaida who was attempting to capture Damascus. On his way back he came to Tadmor (with Islam the town reverted to its ancient name) and laid siege to it. News from Damascus, however, pressed him to raise the siege and move on. The town had not fallen but, as he left, he declared: 'Inhabitants of Tadmor, were you up in the clouds, by God, I will bring you down.'* He left but had not gone far before he was overtaken by a messenger who brought news that the town had surrendered (A.D. 634).

What had happened? Had al Walid left a small force to contain the citizens within the town walls? One can imagine the leaders of the town debating what was the best thing to do. All the country around was teeming with the Moslems who seemed to enjoy phenomenal success. They were in command of all the lands through which trade passed so perhaps the best thing was to surrender and survive rather than resist and be destroyed. There is no evidence of destruction by the al Walid forces, which confirms the idea of voluntary surrender.

The last of the Orthodox Caliphs left the succession wide open. A fierce struggle developed between the rival factions, with the Sunni, Ummayyad family emerging

* Yaqut.

50

triumphant. This family was to establish the Second Caliphate of Islam, a short-lived but pivotal and fascinating national dynasty. They had long been Governors of Damascus during the Orthodox Caliphates and so it was perhaps natural that they should move there the seat of Moslem power. Thus Damascus became the 'capital' of Islam, leaving the old cities of the Orthodox Caliphate in Arabia, Mecca and Medina, as the Holy Cities, the spiritual sources.

Under the Ummayyads Tunisia, Algeria and southern Spain were conquered, as well as Afghanistan. But these far-reaching adventures were of no concern to Tadmor. The Ummayyad love of moving about the land from one fortress palace to another did, however, have direct repercussions on the town. The Caliphs built a considerable number of desert palaces—some of them are small townships such as Anjar in the Bekka of Lebanon—as centres of economic development in areas which were fertile then but which now are in many cases reduced to desert. They were not hunting lodges or desert retreats 'for effete Caliphs' as the romantics would have it. Two of these 'estate centres' were Qasr el Heir West and Qasr el Heir East, both built by Caliph Hisham, lying some forty miles east and west of Tadmor. Hisham's successor, Caliph Walid II, used them frequently but also stayed in Tadmor where he is reported to have lived a debauched life. He was a sensitive poet and lover of the arts, and it was probably an indulgence in cultural activities which were not wholly religious which earned him this reputation amongst the fanatical, proselytising Moslems of the period.

Nonetheless, by the standards of the time Walid II led a debauched life. His cousin, Yazid, son of Walid I, was a far more orthodox Moslem than most of his kinsmen. Accordingly he sent his partisans to dispose of the Caliph whom they ambushed and killed whilst he was out riding near Tadmor.

In the reign of the last Ummayyad Caliph, Marwan II, Tadmor is again mentioned by the Arab chroniclers. The town at that time was governed from Homs by the Banu Kalb—sworn enemies of the Qaisit tribes. Unfortunately the Qaisit supported Marwan, and it looks as though pressure was put on Tadmor, to such an extent that the inhabitants rebelled. The Caliph moved against the town and, having captured it, dismantled the walls. This was recorded by the Abbasid poet, Bashar ibn Burd: 'When came to Palmyra the horses of Qais, then was Palmyra destroyed.' This left the town unprotected, but the fall of the Ummayyad dynasty at the hands of the Abbasids left it even more so.

The new ruling dynasty moved the 'capital' from Damascus to the new city of Baghdad in A.D. 750. No longer was Tadmor near the seat of power, and her gardens and decaying classical splendour went unregarded.

Occasional references occur, such as during the rising against Saif ad Dawla, Emir of Aleppo when the fleeing insurgents were trapped and defeated in Tadmor. But nothing specific enough is given in texts for us to have any idea of the state of its monuments during this period. The town was only a strategic post in the desert and as such it was maintained at little more than subsistence level. The classical ruins were used as quarries for building materials, and a severe earthquake in the tenth century caused further damage.

The Moslem dynasties came and went, the Sanctuary of Bel was fortified, the Temple was made into a mosque. The fortunes of Tadmor rose a little, fell a little, according to the political climate. The Ottomans built a huge castle on a hill overlooking the emaciated city in the late sixteenth century which is still there today, a glowering, menacing steep of walls and towers crowning the slope. Tadmor gradually slipped from town to village, wretched and impoverished, a cluster of mud-brick hovels round the towering, stately walls of the Temple of Bel. The late Arab town was an amorphous mass of mud-brick houses that huddled for support behind the mighty Temenos walls. By the time two Englishmen arrived there in 1751 it was only a wretched hamlet of a few families. The two Englishmen, however, turned the tide and brought the eyes of the world again onto this golden wonder in the desert.

CHAPTER THREE

'Rescue from Oblivion'

PALMYRA slept, folded in the purdah of the desert. Throughout the medieval period there was little interest in classical remains, so that when a Spanish Rabbi, Benjamin of Tudela, visited Tadmor in 1192 his comments on the place excited no attention. At this time, during the Seljuk period, Tadmor was a large township, centred on the fortress Temple of Bel. Benjamin was surprised, and delighted, to find a Jewish community of over two thousand but expressed no enthusiasm for the splendours of ancient architecture around him.

It was to be another five hundred years before a real interest in the classical remains was shown. The English merchant base in Aleppo—they called it a 'factory'—was one of many European 'Khans' in the city. Each country had its Khan or hostelry, allocated by the Sultan in the Frankish quarter, in which the merchants led almost cloistered lives, having little social contact with the Syrian, mostly Moslem population. By 1662 the English Khan, derived from the Levant Company founded by Elizabeth I in 1581, was the most important and numbered as many as fifty merchants. Their existence was precarious but the returns made it worthwhile for those who could accept the deprivations. They had little recreation apart from hunting in the nearby desert, coursing greyhounds, duck-shooting and—no doubt to the utter astonishment of the locals—playing cricket.

It was the merchants at this remote and circumscribed Factory who first ventured out across the desert to reach the ruins about which they had heard such wondrous things. In 1678, Dr Huntington and others set out in high hopes but on this occasion they got rather more—or should one say, 'rather less'?—than they were bargaining for.

> These Gentlemen were no sooner arrived there, at Tadmor, but they fell unhappily into ye hands of a Company of Arabian Robbers, commanded by one Melham, to satisfy whom they were constrained to part with their very clothes; which great loss & ye ffright together so palled their curiosity that they staied not to take more exact survey of ye ancient ruines, but immediately returned home & glad to escape so.*

* *PEQ* (ex *Philosophical Transactions*), Dr Halifax's Report.

Fig. 18 The first pictorial representation of Palmyra; Hofstede's panorama painted shortly after 1691.

One has the hilarious picture of a clutch of portly English merchants scampering across the desert stark naked with a horde of fearsome bedouin bandits hot on their heels.

Having regained their composure—and a new suit of clothes—they settled back into their accustomed ways. Little doubt that the ill-starred expedition was a topic of conversation for quite a while but it soon turned to the possibility of mounting another expedition. 'Since that misfortune though ye voyage had bin often discoursed of yet none had ye courage to undertake it.' This discoursing lasted for thirteen years—which may seem a long time to pluck up enough courage but travel for foreigners outside the well trodden confines of the Levant was a perilous undertaking.

Many travellers even well into the mid-nineteenth century attested to the dangers which could—and probably would—be encountered. However, in 1691 the party decided to venture forth again but this time strong in numbers and 'armed' with a laisez-passer from the tribal sheikh, or ruler, in whose territory Tadmor lay—'having obtained a promise of security from Assine, King of ye Arabs, and one of his own people to shew us ye way, on ye 29th September, 1691, we ventured upon it a second time, making in all frankes and servants about 30 men, well armed'. Europeans living in the Frankish quarter of Aleppo were collectively called Franks.

By 3 October the party had reached the well at Al-withal where in the evening they got caught in a cloudburst. The dried-up wadis in the hills 'were by ye cataracts which descended from ye mountains become rivers', but in a way the

54

storm was a Godsend because by then they were getting low on water and the downpour enabled them to replenish their skins.

The following morning they left Al-withal and headed for 'some of ye ruines of which we pswaded ourselves we could see ye day before, phaps it might be ye castle, which is more than ½ hour distant from ye citty'. After several hours' journey they 'came to ye brow of a rocky Mountain . . . separated from that whereon stands ye Castle of Tadmor, but by a narrow valley'. Here they halted whilst the guide, so solicitously lent them by Assine, King of the Arabs, crept forward to see if the way was clear.

Three or four men were driving their asses towards them and they decided to ask them whether 'ye coast was clear or any of ye Mountain Arabs (were) then at Tadmor or not'. Not surprisingly, however, when thirty well armed franks and servants showed themselves the four poor shepherds 'left their asses, & fled towards ye citty with all speed possible'. They were soon rounded up, however, and brought back to the party where, upon being questioned, they said that there were no mountain arabs in the village at all. The shepherds rejoined their asses and the party set off again towards the castle.

'We could easily discern that it was no old building, retaining no footsteps of ye excellent workmanship & ingenuity of ye antients.' They were told that it had been built by Man Ogle, a Prince of the Druses in the reign of Amurath III who 'flourished' in 1588. Rightly they were a little dubious about this attribution, having never heard of Man Ogle and knowing that the Druse area was in Lebanon. As the drawbridge was no longer there, anyone wanting to inspect the castle had to

Fig. 19 The Sanctuary of Bel before clearance, from a photograph taken by Garstang in the 1920s.

Fig. 20 The Temple of Bel as depicted in Wood and Dawkins's *The Ruins of Palmyra*, published in 1753.

climb up the precipitous face of the rock on which it stood. For all their effort they did not think the inside 'sufficient to recompense ye trouble of getting up to it, ye building being confused, and ye rooms very ill contrived'.

The party then turned their attention to the ruined city which was laid out below them, 'from hence you have ye best prospect of ye country al about: you see Tadmor under you . . .' Time and the desert winds had taken their toll of the city (Fig. 18) so that Dr Halifax and his party were unable to discern any plan or limit for the ruins. They descended the long steep slope and headed for the Sanctuary of Bel where the whole population turned out to stare at them. Population is perhaps a rather grand word because there were only between thirty and forty families living there, 'poor miserable dirty people' living in 'little huts made of dirt within ye walls of a spacious court, which inclosed a most magnificent heathen Temple' (Fig. 19).

Thanks to their guide, who was known to the inhabitants, they were welcomed and conducted through the fortified entrance to the sheikh's house where they were to be accommodated. They then set out to explore the Sanctuary. Nowhere before had they come across such a mixture of 'ye greatest state and magnificence together with ye extremity of filth & poverty'. They measured the Temenos wall and commented upon the architectural treatment which exactly accords with

56

what we see today. They recognised the fortress as being on the site, and partly incorporating the ancient propylaea, commenting on 'many pillars broken or sawed asunder being rolled into ye ffabrick but ill cemented'. This 'pillar' bastion still stands (Fig. 45).

One of the results of their visit was the first series of Greek inscriptions from Palmyra. They were also the first to be confronted by the Palmyrene alphabet and of course did not recognise it; however, they made one or two copies of the script which introduced it to western scholarship. Inspecting the propylaea/fortress, they noticed an inscription on a stone above the entrance: 'Over this little door there is an Inscription in Greek, & also another in another language & character, which I never saw til in Tadmor.' This stone was evidently re-used from somewhere else by Abdul Hassan Yussuf ibn Fairouz who fortified the whole sanctuary in 1132: but by curious chance it happened to be a memorial inscription to Septimius Odainat. Queen Zenobia was a legend, but their excitement would have been intense had they realised that this inscription probably related to her husband.

They recorded that only fifty-eight pillars were still standing in the Temenos, approximately the same number as today. Of those surrounding the temple itself there were sixteen standing whereas today there are only eight. The drawings done by Borra for Wood and Dawkins almost a century later show three pillars with full entablature at the north-west corner (Fig. 20) together with at least two pillars on the south side. The eastern flank is indicated to have been almost completely intact and with pillars on either side of the entrance portal. One can be fairly sure that these pillars were standing at the time of Dr Halifax's visit because they are also discernible in the painting (Fig. 18) by G. Hofstede van Essen, a Dutch artist who was a member of the party. It was at this time that Hofstede made a detailed drawing of the ruins which he later worked up into a full scale painting. This was probably done at the house of Coenraat Calckbrenner, the Dutch consul in Aleppo, from where it went to Amsterdam. It now hangs in the Hall of Amsterdam University. It is the oldest representation of the ruins and as such is a vital piece of evidence in the study of Palmyra.

Dr Halifax was greatly impressed by the Temple of Bel and the luxuriant carvings which he saw. His description is delightfully enthusiastic: 'by ye small remains yet to be seen (the temple) seems to have bin one of ye most glorious structures in ye world: I never saw clusters of grapes so bold (Fig. 8), so lively, so natural in any place'. Apart from one or two eagle carvings (see page 122) about which they conjectured rather wildly, he noticed the 'most curious ffret work & carvings' in the ceiling of the north adyton of the Temple 'in ye midst of which is a Domo or cupola above 6 foot diameter'. He also noted that it was a monolith and wondered whether so large a stone could have been 'made of some artificial cement or composition by time hardened into a lapideous substance'. This ceiling is the famous Zodiac ceiling (see page 122) (Fig. 62).

Having inspected and measured the Temple and its Temenos, and taken note of several inscriptions, they went out into the ruined city 'where our eyes were presently arrested with an amazing sight of a multitude of marble pillars' (Fig. 21). Then as now the lasting impression of Palmyra is that of a city of pillars. He and his party were bowled over by the place and eulogised over it. 'You have ye prospect of such magnificent ruines, yet if it be lawful to frame a conjecture (a thing he was doing all the time) of ye original beauty of ye place by what is still remaining I question whether any citty in ye world could have challenged precedence of this in its glory.'

The Monumental Arch sent Dr Halifax into further raptures: 'A magnificent entrance vastly large, & for ye exquisiteness of ye workmanship, nothing inferior to any thing before described, I wish I could ad that it had not suffered ye same fate with ye rest, & then we might have seen a rare piece of ye antient beauty of ye place.' He then mistook the first existing leg of the Colonnade Street to be a 'noble piazza' with one hundred and twenty-nine pillars still standing 'intire'. He noted that 'upon almost all ye pillars we found inscriptions both in Greek and ye language unknown'; there are few instances of a single language inscription. This

Fig. 21 Part of the panorama from
The Ruins of Palmyra.

59

bilingual manner of inscriptions enabled the Doctor, who had a good command of Greek, to fathom out that these were inscriptions to help people whom the city wished to honour: 'ye state & ye people did sometimes honour those that had bin in public trusts, with inscriptions upon these pillars . . . Upon several of these pillars, are little pedestals jetting out, sometimes one way only, sometimes more, which seem to have bin ye bases or standing places of statues but none of these are remaining . . . (they were) put up in memory of some who have behaved themselves in those public offices which they bore, either in their own Republick, or under ye Romans which commendation, this being a publick place were their names & publick actions recorded & so transmitted to Posterity.'

Even with his knowledge there were many problems which the inscriptions could not help solve. There were in fact a few texts which only a knowledge of Parthian and Sassanian history could help explain. At that time, the Parthians were little more than a name to scholars—a name oft repeated in Roman texts but referring to a place and people about whom virtually nothing was known. Of 'Olgassus' (sic) 'I am unwilling to entertain any thoughts' for understandably he had never heard of Vologasias, the new Parthian capital founded on the Tigris to compete with and waste the Hellenistic city of Seleucia.

Of the Baths of Diocletian he noted 'ye ruines of a very stately building . . . (which) is built of better marble, & hath an air of delicacy & exquisiteness in ye work beyond what is discernable in ye Piazza'. He measured the porphyry pillars, noted the inscription (one of the few in Latin) on the entablature and recorded: 'In these ruines we found ye only latrine.' Why is it that visitors to Roman ruins always look for, and expect to find, a latrine?

He also seems to have taken the south side of the Colonnade Street to have been the pillared front of a palace with 'several openings for gates leading into ye court of ye palace'. One of these courts must surely have been the Tariff Court or the Agora. A slight problem is raised, however, by a comment that some of the pillars had plain or smooth shafts whilst 'some wrought & channeld as those in ye Temple'. The pillars of the Temple of Bel are certainly fluted with blind fluting in the lower parts, but there are no fluted pillars in the Colonnade Street.

The party then visited Ain Efqa, the waters of which they found quite drinkable: 'under ye long walke, runs a current of hot sulphorous waters . . . and it is still used by ye people of ye country to bath in'. Obviously they had come across hot springs before in Syria—indeed Dr Halifax says they are very frequently found—but 'The scent of ye waters here is much like those of ye Bath in England, but not so strong, neither is ye taste so offensive on ye contrary when they have run in ye aqua-duct so far from ye fountain as to become cold, they are very potable, & are ye only waters ye habitants use.'

They were totally unprepared for the Valley of Tombs. 'But as great a curiosity

Fig. 22 The Valley of the Tombs from *The Ruins of Palmyra*.

as any were their sepulchres, being square towers 4 or 5 stories high and standing on bothe sides of a hollow way ... stretching for about a mile.'

Living in an alien culture perhaps there was some comfort at the sudden prospect of finding a church spire—however improbable the likelihood may seem. 'Some thought them (the ruined tower tombs) ye steeples of ruined churches, & were in hopes we should have found some footsteps of Christianity here.' Alas, not churches—although there is still one today which looks like a spire when seen from afar (Wiegand No. 9)—but a necropolis. Close inspection, however, revealed what they were. They saw quite a few (Fig. 22) comparing their relative magnificence: 'they were all of ye same form but of different splendour & greatness according to ye circumstances of ye founder'. This is very true. They understood the tiers of loculi and were also struck by the sculptures: 'they are 2 square towers rather larger than an ordinary steeple, & 5 stories high, ye outside being of common stone, but ye partitions & floors within of marble & beautified too with very lively carvings & paintings, & figures both of men and women as far as ye breast & shoulders, but miserably defaced & broken'. A recumbent group—possibly the one on the Tomb of Kithoth (Fig. 1) which was later to feature in a Wood and Dawkins drawing (Fig. 132)—caught their eye: 'one of a man & another of a woman, cut in a sitting or rather leaning posture'.

However, they were getting nervous and wanted to be away. They had stayed four days, 'rumaging' amongst the ruins and recording inscriptions, but were in constant fear of the nomadic bedouin—the 'Mountain Arabs'—who had so unceremoniously despatched the first party of explorers thirteen years earlier. '... thinking it not safe to linger too long in a place, where should ye Mountain Arabs who are enemies to Assine Abas our friend, have intelligence of us, they might either fall upon or endeavour to intercept us in our return, for which reason also we had all along concealed our intended course, under a pretence of proceeding for Damascus...' They were, however, 'well pleased with what we had seen, & glad to escape so dread a place without any trouble or pretence upon us, but else with some regret for having left a great many things behind which deserved a more particular & curious inspection'.

They journeyed on, heading for home. They met and were entertained by 'King' Assine who showed them great hospitality and friendship. Dr Halifax does, at this point in his narrative, make one particular comment which is illuminating. It highlights the attitude of even friendly Arabs to visitors in these remote sites. '... before supper ye King himself made us a visit in person bidding us wellcome to Fay (where he was encamped) & asked what we had seen in our travels that pleased us? how we liked Tadmor? & whether we had found a treasure there? for this notion stickes in ye heads of all these people, that the Frankes goe to see old Ruines only because there they meet with Inscriptions which direct them to some hid treasure, & therefore tis no unusual thing with them, when they find a stone with an inscription on one side to turn it down to ye ground, that it might not be seen or read by any: But we assured him we went with no such Expectation, but only out of a desire to see ye place; neither had we brought anything away with us but a piece of porphyry stone which upon his request we shewed him...' The poor King, he must have thought them out of their minds.

Dr Halifax's report is the first important comment on Palmyra since its passing from the western scene. Unscientific and lacking in any detailed comment on the architecture it may be, but it gives a picture of the ruins, and much else besides, at that period. Considering the time available and the circumstances under which it was written, the journal is a remarkable achievement. The report is a document not without humour and one which, whilst recognising the perils, in no way over-dramatises them or seeks to present the travellers as heroes. *Relation of a Voyage to Tadmor* was published in 1695 in *The Philosophical Transactions of the Royal Society* by 'Dr William Halifax, of C.C.C., Oxon., Chaplain to the Factory at Aleppo'.

The next report, likewise, offered little informed architectural criticism. It was

Fig. 23 Part of the panorama of the ruined city in which Wood and Dawkins depicted architectural fragments heaped—almost as though artistically arranged—so that their details are clearly shown.

by a gentleman architect called Cornelius Loos, attached to the staff of King Charles XII of Sweden who at that time was conducting his Poltavian campaign. When Charles was besieged by the Turks at Bender, Loos was with him and became his constant companion. In March 1710, Charles sent him to Egypt, Palestine and Syria to draw pictures of the ancient monuments in those countries.

What survives of his report (part of it was lost in the battle at Bender in 1711) is like Dr Halifax's, a general survey. The main importance of it lies today in the drawing which shows that much has been lost; even complete structures have vanished. It is not possible, therefore, to identify everything.

Despite the trouble and dangers entailed in reaching Tadmor, travellers were still attracted by the fabulous ruins. Europe still had no clear idea of what the architecture was like: all that the earliest artists, Hofstede and Loos, had shown was a bewildering array of rubble lying, as though artistically arranged, or newly fallen (Fig. 23).

Fig. 24 Robert Wood (*left*), painted by Allan Ramsay, and James Dawkins (*right*) from a pencil and pastel by James 'Athenian' Stuart.

This was soon to alter, for in 1751 two Englishmen, Robert Wood and James Dawkins (Fig. 24, see also Fig. 35) visited the site and made detailed drawings of all the most important monuments as well as an impressive collection of sculptured architectural details. They had the help of an Italian architect called Giovanni Battista Borra whom they recruited in Rome where Wood and Dawkins spent the winter of 1749/50. It was Borra's job to make the minutely detailed drawings which were eventually published in 1753. The publication of *The Ruins of Palmyra* had an immediate and far-reaching effect on architectural taste and development in England. This is discussed in the next chapter; here we are concerned with the travellers themselves.

The Middle East was no new ground to Wood for he had already been there as early as 1743. In 1749 he accepted Dawkins's invitation to join him on a tour of Asia Minor, with the express intention of making architectural drawings of hitherto undocumented sites. This, it was felt, 'might produce amusement and improvement to ourselves as well as some advantage to the publick'. They had before them the fact 'that the measures of the antient buildings of Rome (drawn) by Monsieur Desgodetz have been of the greatest use'. And so they set out to 'rescue from oblivion the magnificence of Palmyra'.

The year 1749 was spent in Asia Minor inspecting a formidable list of antique monuments. It must be remembered that at this time knowledge and some competence in architecture was considered a necessary part of a gentleman's education. By this classical architecture was meant. But by 1750 horizons and architectural interests were broadening and men who swayed taste were drawing on stimuli and inspiration from sources further and further afield. To meet this ever-increasing need men with adventurous spirits were braving the 'Mountain Arabs' and heading for Greece, Asia Minor and the Levant. So it was that James Dawkins, son of a wealthy Jamaican merchant, with the practised Wood at his side, toured the Eastern Mediterranean. In 1751, after a considerable amount of preparation—which everyone had to go through right up to the 1920s—they managed to reach the ruined Palmyra where they stayed for two weeks.

Getting there had not been easy. Everyone still dreaded the 'Mountain Arabs' who had put Dr Halifax into such a quiver. Not even the Pasha in Damascus had any authority over them. 'The Bashaw (Pasha) of this city told us, he could not promise that his name, or power, would be any security to us in the place we were going.' However he advised them to go and see the 'Aga' of a village to the north who obviously had influence with the Bedouin. So they sought out the Aga of Hassia and then set out on 11 March 'with an escort of the Aga's best Arab horsemen, armed with guns and long pikes' (Fig. 132). Their caravan numbered over two hundred persons and about the same number of animals. On the third day 'our guide told us, this part of our journey was most dangerous, and desired we might submit ourselves entirely to his direction, which was, that the servants should keep with the baggage immediately behind our Arab guard; from which one, two or more of their body were frequently dispatched, for discovery, to what ever eminences they could see, where they remained until we came up. Those horsemen always rode off from the caravan at full speed, in the Tartar and Husiar manner. We doubted whether all this precaution was owing to their being really apprehensive of danger, or whether they only affected to make us think highly of their use and vigilance.'

Eventually they came through the hills which guard the city, 'when the hills opening discovered to us, all at once, the greatest quantity of ruins we had ever seen, all of white marble, and beyond them towards the Euphrates a flat waste, as far as the eye could reach, without any object which shewed either life or motion. It is scarce possible to imagine anything more striking than this view: So great a number of Corinthian pillars, mixed with so little wall or solid building, afforded a most romantic variety of prospect.'

It was not all sightseeing; indeed it must have been a very hard-working visit, as they set-to to record in marvellous detail the sumptuous architecture they saw before them. They worked under the greatest difficulties, being bothered by the local people who still thought they were treasure-seekers. This suspicion made life hazardous for countless scholars, as Robin Fedden has pointed out: 'Accused of digging for treasure when they were mapping ancient sites, robbed of their scientific instruments which were thought to be magical apparatus, these early travellers rediscovered Syria and the Levant in difficult circumstances.'* When Wood and Dawkins, with the aid of the talented Mr Borra, started measuring, they must have appeared to the locals as the proverbial treasure-hunters but using a new Frankish way of divining the hiding place of the booty of history.

Their patience and bravery were amply rewarded when they got back to England and published the results of their work. The Report written by Wood solicited the most enthusiastic praise from that arbiter of English taste, Horace Walpole: 'Of all the works that distinguish this age, none perhaps excel those beautiful editions of Baalbeck and Palmyra.' Later Gibbons was to add his thunder to the applause over 'the magnificent descriptions and drawings of Dawkins and Wood, who have transported into England the ruins of Palmyra and Baalbeck'. It should be added that on their way home they visited Baalbeck and conducted a similar measuring exercise amid the towering ruins of Baalbeck in the Bekka. *The Ruins of Palmyra* enjoyed an enormous success. A Paris edition was brought out at the same time which even reached the Court of Catherine the Great in St Petersburg. The French enclave there immediately christened her capital 'the Palmyra of the North', no doubt equating Catherine with the fabulous Queen Zenobia. Despite this sycophantic humbug, there was another Zenobia lined up for Palmyra, an English noblewoman.

She was one of the most extraordinary, indeed almost bizarre, women ever to have turned the pages of Middle Eastern history. A self-willed and disillusioned aristocrat with unshakeable self-confidence and an imperturbable sense of authority, Lady Hester Stanhope burst upon the Levant, defying both social and religious taboos, making herself a legend about whom the hard facts are infinitely more interesting than the legion of scandals and hearsay that have accumulated about her memory.

It would be easy to write off Lady Hester as a stupid and reckless libertine but this, like most of the stories about her, would be both untrue and unfair. Unconventional she certainly was, but her achievement amongst the Arabs of the desert, with the Ottoman authorities and finally with the Druses on Mount Lebanon, was something no conventional character could have managed.

A straightforward explanation of her character is not possible. She was one of

* *Syria and Lebanon.*

the most eccentric and singular women travellers ever to have lived, even in a century which was to produce a rich crop of like persons. Her life in England had, however, started against a very conventional background. She was a grand-daughter of the great Chatham, her mother was the clever sister of William Pitt, and was born in the beautiful Palladian house at Chevening in Kent, with its leafy, dream-like park stretching into ordered rural calm. Nonetheless, she enjoyed all the privileges and upbringing of a woman of her class. The tomboy who once said she was going to cross over to France in a rowing boat, grew up to become for a while William Pitt's official hostess. Thus she came into contact with all the most prominent men and minds of her day. She was no mute decoration on the official and social scene, no simpering hostess who made all the right banal noises at the appropriate moments without having anything worthwhile to say. She had personality and a mind of her own which she held against the odds of some of the best brains in London. In later years, in Constantinople, Canning found her 'measureless exuberance' and the 'not infrequent singularities' of her conversation both stimulating and exhausting. She loved being at the centre of things, playing the leading part. As hostess to her uncle, she could only find partial satisfaction, and London Society, with its fluttering hostesses, began to pall rather quickly.

She was certainly very close to her uncle and between them there was real affection. When he died she felt isolated, which only aggravated an inborn loneliness. How to console herself? To throw herself into the whirl of London Society with its narrow horizons and foppery, would have irritated her beyond measure.

Pitt's death released her pent-up romanticism and in 1810 she took off for the Eastern Mediterranean. By now this region was considered hugely romantic, with wild, untamed landscapes peopled with dark-eyed sheikhs wrapped up in voluminous cloaks, charging about on superb thoroughbred stallions through the decaying pillars of lost and ancient cities. There was the evening call to prayer as the sun sank from a limpid and darkening sky slowly towards the west, when mysterious holy cities were hushed by devotion and the falling night. The danger and the dirt were ignored and a magical fantasy reality, in which the simple life amid simple people, assumed a glamour that made the sophistication of London seem trivial and artificial.

Pitt had left her £1,500 a year—later to be reduced to £1,200—and this she spent liberally. She did not succeed in pulling the wool over the eyes of Kinglake (who was as incurable a romantic as the rest) for he immediately realised that 'a longing for the East very commonly felt by proud people when goaded by sorrow' was the real prompt for her Mediterranean visit. When she arrived in Constantinople he could have no idea of what lay ahead of her. He also realised that it was quite useless trying to control her, for, as Pitt had said, 'I let her do as she pleases; for if she were resolved to cheat the devil she could do it . . .'

67

PALMYRA

After Constantinople she and her small party set out for Cairo, arriving there in 1811. The core of this party consisted of Lady Hester herself and her ever-faithful maid, a young gentleman, Michael Bruce, who was both escort and lover, and Dr Meryon, a physician who remained with her and looked after her throughout her long stay in the Middle East. Around this quartet she assembled a vast retinue of servants, guards, guides and 'friends', all of whom were paid, clustering round the queen bee so long as the honey lasted. Much of the huge expense of all this was paid for by Michael Bruce's father. In the beginning he probably approved of his son's alliance with so noted and well-connected a lady, seeing in their association the main chance of a glowing political career for his son. In any case travel would broaden his mind, whilst the company of such a woman would give him polish and manners as well as tune up his wits. As her escort, with the faithful and eminently respectable Dr Meryon ever present, to say nothing of the maid, young Bruce represented no reflection on her honour. That Society knew exactly what was going on was neither here nor there; form had been observed and Society in England was not outraged—only twitching with excitement as rumour and speculation cloaked the debacle with an ever-thickening blanket of myth.

The year 1812 saw the party, plus the multitudinous caravan of hangers-on, in Sidon. It was a triumphal procession, with Lady Hester queening it over all and every occasion. She was neither beautiful nor pretty but had a nobility and presence which quickly commanded respect. She also had courage, generosity and boundless self-confidence. These, added to a dauntless will and contempt for obstacles—and a seemingly bottomless purse—were the basis of her success in Syria. That she succeeded in a fanatically Moslem and anti-feminist country like Syria, is all the more remarkable. Her fellow countrymen were continually advising her to take care, but this was almost a way of ensuring that she did whatever she was advised not to do.

The extravagant caravan caused excitement enough as it rolled its stately way across the hills and valleys of the Levant, but the first real gasp of astonishment from Franks and Arabs alike came when she rode into holy Damascus (from which even Consuls were still debarred) and visited the Pasha by night. In an enthusiastic letter to Canning she wrote: 'My visit to the Pasha of Damascus in the night during Ramadan was the finest thing possible. I was mounted on an Arab horse he had given me, my people on foot and he (the Pasha) surrounded by two thousand servants and picked guards.' 'My people'! Who did she think she was? A queen on a state progress, quite possibly. Robin Fedden has put it well: 'Incorrigibly romantic, she was infected, like so many after her, by the glamour of the Arab world. Perhaps even more important, she was something of a megalomaniac. Difficult and self-obsessed, she could bear neither contradiction nor rivalry.

Chatham's grand-daughter would divide the honours with no-one; she needed a stage to herself, and in Syria she found it.'*

It was probably in Damascus that she seized upon the idea of a spectacular visit to Palmyra. Dr Meryon may have touched fairly near the mark when, later in life, he wrote about his strange years with Lady Hester. Her motive for the journey was not just a display of head-strong recklessness, it was all tied up with her sexual repression, her vision of herself as a woman who could defy and conquer the restrictions which her age and society saw fit to impose on the 'weaker sex', and the fact that for her Zenobia had triumphed in similar circumstances. 'But, besides the wish to behold broken columns and dilapidated temples, Lady Hester may be supposed to have had other motives peculiar to herself ... These columns and temples owed the greatest part of their magnificence to one of her own sex, whose talents and whose fate, remotely akin to her own, no doubt might move her sympathy so far as to prompt her to visit the spot which a celebrated woman had governed. She sought the remains of Zenobia's greatness, as well as the remains of Palmyra.'†

Whatever the motive, everyone, Pasha, friends, officials and Franks were appalled at the notion and urged her to abandon the idea. And as the opposition stiffened so did her resolve. No white woman had ever been to Tadmor, had she not heard of the horrifying things which had happened to other travellers? It was a fantastic and impossible scheme so she couldn't be serious and certainly must not go.

The whole petrified caravan set out for Palmyra in March 1813, with proud, obdurate Lady Hester mounted on the Pasha's horse leading the way quite unperturbed. She had never dealt with intermediaries, she always went direct to the person with the actual power or authority. The fact that the Bedouin of the desert did not acknowledge the authority of the Damascus government only meant that she, Lady Hester Stanhope, would deal direct with them.

The ever-patient Dr Meryon had been despatched on a preliminary reconnaissance to Palmyra, an unpleasant undertaking which, however, he achieved with considerable success. On the first visit in January he was not particularly impressed by the ruins, which seemed small against the magnificence of the surrounding hills. 'Yet, when we reflect on the vastness of the materials which have been collected, as it were, in the midst of the desert, we are lost in astonishment. There are pillars of granite of a single block, which (say those who have made researches on these subjects their study) must have been transported from Upper Egypt....' How right the doctor was: this comment about granite columns shows how much the state of knowledge regarding antiquities had progressed since the day of Dr Halifax when no such deduction would have been possible. Having selected a 'cottage' in the north-west part of the Temenos of the Temple of Bel, where the Arab village was to be found, he went for a swim in Ain Efqa, and then set off back to Damascus.

'Having satisfied Lady Hester on the practicability of her journey to Palmyra ...', the whole great caravan had set out across the desert. 'Seldom, too, was witnessed a caravan of a few individuals on a more magnificent scale ... Twenty-two camels were to bear the tents, luggage, firewood, rice, flour, tobacco, coffee, sugar, soap, saucepans, spare horseshoes, and other provisions; eight carried water and nine corn for the horses. We were escorted by guard of Bedouin, headed by a prince's son; and our own cavalcade amounted to twenty-five horsemen ...' This escort had cost her—or rather Michael Bruce's father—the considerable sum of £150.

She looked upon her entry into Palmyra as the greatest triumph of her life. 'I carried everything before me, and was crowned under the triumphal arch ...' Well, not quite. Her entry into Palmyra was certainly a rural spectacle and the Arabs put on a good show. But Dr Meryon's description of the event is a little more down to earth. 'The inhabitants resolved on welcoming Lady Hester in the best manner they could, and had gone out in a body to meet her ...' There was much rushing about on horses and firing of guns. For her amusement they put on a demonstration of an attack and defence of a caravan, an act executed with such gusto that Dr Meryon was tempted at certain moments to suspect that it was going to become the real thing. Then 'The men on foot exhibited on the person of a horseman the mode of stripping for plunder, and no *valet de chambre* could undress his master more expeditiously.' The whole cortege then went down the Valley of Tombs, where Lady Hester showed great interest in the monuments, and so on into the ruined city. With a fine sense of occasion they led her down the Colonnade Street, 'In order to increase the effect.' As they neared the Arch they noted that on the brackets jutting out from the pillars young girls had been placed 'in the most graceful postures, and with garlands in their hands; their elegant shapes but slightly concealed by a single loose robe, girded at the waist with a zone, and a white crape veil covering their heads ...' When the party arrived at the Arch all the girls jumped down and danced round her, leading her on towards the Temple of Bel where she was welcomed by the entire population: '... bearded elders chanted verses in her praise and all the spectators joined in chorus ...' She was taken to her 'cottage' in the Temenos where she rested.

What really must she have thought? Was it really her crowning triumph? She had been a part of a real spectacle when she was received by the Pasha in Damascus and therefore knew something of the splendour which could be mounted. There she had been accommodated in a beautiful house in Damascus and feted most charmingly. Here in Palmyra she was greeted by a depleted tribe of

Fig. 25 The arrival of Lady Hester Stanhope in Palmyra—from Dr Meryon's *Travels of Lady Hester Stanhope* published in 1846.

poor desert people and was accommodated in a mud-brick hovel despite Dr Meryon's description of it as a 'cottage'. News of the event spread like wildfire and soon became elaborated far beyond its real truth. For a woman who had known the flood-lights of the big stage with all its gorgeous trappings, this must have been a pretty tatty affair. The contemporary drawing of her arrival at her 'cottage' (Fig. 25) has a thinly populated and slightly pathetic effect and is probably more true of the circumstances than all the richly ornamented stories recounted later. No-one would ever know what a dispiriting affair it really had been: like the Divine Sarah playing to a half-filled house in a repertory theatre in some seedy Midland town. The legend was the important thing, but how sad for her.

The expense, not only of the visit to Palmyra but of the whole Levantine expedition, had been enormous and Michael Bruce's father felt he could no longer afford it. It was obvious by now that this aimless meander about the Levant could go on forever, and with the tales now being told in London of their bohemian and scandalous way of life, the old man presumably thought that enough was enough for his son. The young man was persuaded to return to England and follow some respectable livelihood. With his departure Lady Hester was deprived of a considerable slice of her income and so she retired to a deserted convent, first at Mar Elias near Saida, and latterly to one near the village of Jouni not far away.

She still kept up a lively interest in Levant affairs, sending advice to Pashas, officials and consuls on any subject which took her fancy. Until the end of her life she was revered by the people and was treated by officialdom with a curious combination of genuine respect and bewildered affection. They all found her persistent interference in affairs irksome but she had shown her ability to command and rule, so they left her undisturbed in her hill-top convent. There she was hostess to every famous traveller of her age.

Towards the end of her life she became more and more of a recluse, receiving only in the twilight so that no-one should see how her face was ageing. It was a sad fizzling out of a bright spark. But she had been born with a disastrous combination of powerful characteristics which, had she also mastered restraint and self-control, might have shaped her into one of the great figures of her time. The tragedy of Lady Hester Stanhope was that so much outstanding talent was wasted on display and a fruitless egotism.

The journals kept by tourists contributed very little to our knowledge of the place. For the most part they were travelogues for the use of those who followed in their footsteps. In mid-Victorian times one of the most popular guide books was the one published by two Royal Naval captains, the Hon. C. L. Irby and Mr J. Mangles. These two officers spent a great deal of time during 1817 and 1818 touring about the Middle East and becoming involved in all sorts of adventures and happenings. They were on the Nile when their friend Mr Bankes bagged the hieroglyph obelisk from Philae which he was later to erect in the gardens of his country house at Kingston Lacey in Dorset (where it still stands). They helped excavate the entrance to the temples at Abu Simbel, appeared in Petra only a few years after Burckhardt had rediscovered it, in fact kept on turning up in all the most unlikely places. Visitors in the backwoods of the Middle East were still a great rarity, and those who did venture forth were really quite intrepid. None more so than Irby and Mangles who, dressed as Arabs (or rather their romantic notion of what an Arab should look like), braved the considerable risks of travel in the area. Some idea of the dangers can be gained by the fact that as late as 1912 travellers to Palmyra were advised by the ubiquitous Baedeker Guide to take an armed escort.

Irby and Mangles, however, could be pretty scathing about some of the ancient sites, and Palmyra caught the full blast of their opprobrium: '... not a single column, pediment, architrave, portal or frieze worthy of admiration...' They also disliked the statuary brackets on the pillars, 'The projecting pedestals in the centre of the columns of the great avenue have a very unsightly appearance....' whilst the Monumental Arch '... so beautiful on paper, is excessively insignificant in reality; and the decorated frieze is very badly wrought: even the devices are not striking'. They harped on the lack of size of the columns compared with those at Baalbeck, in fact they did not think much of Palmyra. Rather grudgingly they had to admit that 'The plates of Wood and Dawkins are certainly well executed, but they have done more than justice to the originals.' But all was not lost on them; they found the Valley of Tombs very interesting and were 'much struck with the picturesque effect of the whole mass, presenting altogether the most imposing sight of the kind we had ever seen....' Their final judgement on the place was, however, far from encouraging: '... we judged Palmyra to be hardly worthy of the time, expense, anxiety and the fatiguing journey ... we suspect that it was the difficulties of getting to Tadmor and the fact that few travellers have been there, that has given rise to the great renown of the ruins.'*

Wood and Dawkins had set in train an interest in Palmyra which was not to die. In consequence scholars now turned their attentions to the site. Volney visited in 1787 and L.–F. Cassas in the 1790s when he made a series of pictorial drawings which are still informative today (Figs. 26, 93, 135 and 138). The Marquis de Vogüé came in 1853 and put his formidable talents at deciphering inscriptions to work. He was followed in 1861 by Waddington who collected more than one hundred previously unrecorded inscriptions. It is upon the researches of these and others that much of our historical knowledge of Palmyra now rests.

It was not, however, until the dawn of the twentieth century that systematic and scientific archaeological excavations really began. Up until this time Palmyra had been a happy hunting ground for souvenir collectors on the grand scale. Not that Palmyra was alone in this respect; the classical remains within the Ottoman Empire were plundered—if that is the right word—either on behalf of wealthy European patrons or for the newly emerging national museums. It can be argued that had these treasures been left where they were they might well not have survived to the present day. But robbery of ancient sites (Fig. 26), not backed by a worthwhile and scholarly spirit of enquiry, had accelerated to a terrifying pace. As Rostovtzeff put it, 'In a few decades scarcely a column or an arch would have been left standing on the site....'† One has the fanciful picture of merchants and tourists trudging across the desert laden with whole sections of buildings or façades. But is it really that fanciful for there is a sizeable portion of Severan Leptis Magna standing romantically rearranged as a 'ruin' beside the lake at Virginia Water in Windsor Great Park, whilst the entire huge Gate to the South Market of Miletus is in the Pergamon Museum in Berlin.

The Russian Archaeological Institute in Constantinople was the first on the scene in 1900 under the direction of a formidable battery of scholars. Their interest might have been prompted to some extent by their involvement in shipping the famous Palmyra Tariff to St Petersburg, and by the publication of Prince Abamelek Lazareff's book on Palmyra in 1884. The Excavation Report of the Institute was the first real meat of archaeology in Palmyra, but it is to the German Archaeological Mission which worked there between 1902 and 1917 that we owe the framework in which all subsequent investigations have taken place. This

* Irby and Mangles, *Travels etc.*   † *Caravan Cities.*

Fig. 26 An engraving after a drawing by L.–F. Cassas showing tomb robbers looting the Tower Tomb of Kithoth: a romantic view but with remarkably accurate architectural detail.

Mission, under the direction of one of the great names of Levant archaeology, Theodor Wiegand, mapped the whole site, photographed and measured each monument in detail and gave each tomb a number. All this work was published in two volumes in Berlin in 1933—*Palmyra, Ergebnisse der Expeditionen von 1902 und 1917*—which are still of fundamental importance to archaeologists today.

For the German scholars the work in hand was a scientific operation which required its own serious language and factual mode of expression: not the faintest personal glimmer comes through the text. Science had taken over from romance and they were suitably matter of fact. There are no twists of humour nor the slightest glint of excitement; they remained unmoved either by beauty or by ugliness. Nonetheless their Report is a massive work of scholarship undertaken in the nick of time.

After the First World War, Palmyra saw a great deal of activity with such great names as Seyrig, Cantineau, Amy, Starcky working on the site. They opened the door to the world, indeed it was an American Professor from Yale University, Ingholdt, who first classified Palmyrene sculpture.

During the Second World War, the Middle East was a highly sensitive area. In May 1941, a German-inspired rebellion against the British Government in Iraq took place, and the R.A.F. base at Habbaniya was invested by the Iraqi Army led by a junta of pro-German officers. A British force crossed the desert between Palestine and Iraq and relieved Habbaniya. It then marched on Baghdad, which two days later surrendered, and the rebellion was put down.

However, in other parts of the country, which included most of the oil-producing regions, the rebellion lingered on and flying columns were despatched to mop up these areas. One of these was the border with Syria, which was controlled by the Vichy French. At about this time the Germans started to use various airfields in Syria with the agreement of the Vichy French, against British operations in the Middle East: Palmyra was one of these bases. The danger of this situation provoked the British Government to invade Syria. The main advance was up from Palestine but as there was already a force operating in Western Iraq it was ordered to advance into Syria along the Euphrates and Tripoli oil pipeline. This T (Tripoli) line had along its route a number of pumping stations: one of these was at Palmyra (see page 208).

Lt. A. V. Wellesley (now the 8th Duke of Wellington), Royal Horse Guards, was serving with the column advancing up the 'T' line towards Palmyra. On 22 June they ran into heavy French Air Force activity with bombing and machine-gun fire from fighters. All his vehicles were hit but they reached both the pumping station (nominated T.3) as well as the aerodrome. Lt. Wellesley described the day in his notes as 'Black Sunday'.

The next day they moved into the hills to the north of the town despite the bombing attacks which started early. The air situation was relieved by the arrival of British Tomahawks, long range R.A.F. fighters sent from Palestine, which shot down six French bombers. Nonetheless the picture was not good because their supply columns had been cut and they were short of food and water. Lt. Wellesley went up to the top of one of the hills and looked down on the ruins through which he was to lead a fighting patrol. It was much as Dr Halifax had done in 1691: '. . . from hence you have ye best prospect of ye country al about: you see Tadmor under you . . .'

Supply lines were re-established and after a few days he was ordered to take his patrol of about twenty men into the ruins after dark. They were to see whether the ruins were patrolled by the French at night and to reconnoitre the road on the far side. 'We slipped across the no-man's-land between our position and the ruins, undetected, at about midnight. We made a thorough reconnaissance of the ruins without encountering any French troops, and reached the road on the far side. As far as I can remember we cut the telephone lines on this road, and presume the object of this was to make communications more difficult for the French. The road appeared to be still in use, presumably to supply the town from the west.

'After reaching the road we turned back through the ruins, located the various French outposts on the western outskirts of the town where we saw in the half light a certain amount of enemy activity and obvious indications of a dawn patrol. We then made our way back across the no-man's-land as it was getting light. Our orders were to do this so that we should not be detected by the enemy troops holding the castle to the west of the ruins.' They were detected but the fire was so ineffective that no harm came of it.

The ruins by moonlight are fascinatingly ethereal yet slightly sinister in their still silence, and one can appreciate the 'incredible impression' they left on Lt. Wellesley's mind. Add to this the tense atmosphere under which the patrol was conducted and we have one of the most unusual visits ever made to the ruins: 'My own impression however, of the night was how incredible, if somewhat eerie, the ruins looked in the moonlight ...'*

A day or two afterwards his Regiment continued its advance westwards leaving Palmyra to surrender to the Essex Regiment shortly afterwards.

With the end of hostilities and the end of the French Syrian Mandate, the Syrian Directorate of Antiquities and Museums took on the huge task of co-ordinating excavations sponsored by the great international foundations as well as implementing site researches on their own behalf. 1954 to 1956 saw a Swiss Mission at work under Professor Collart, whilst a Polish team under Professor Michalowski has progressed uninterrupted with excavations particularly at the Camp of Diocletian, and with spectacular results.

With all these scholars moving in and out, digging here and there, it is surprising that when one visits Palmyra there hardly ever seems to be anyone about. Occasionally a goatherd will drive his flock between some pillars, the goat bells round their necks clunking discordantly, or a posse of tourists will disgorge from a bus and be lost from sight in seconds. No doubt they are somewhere, cameras clicking hard, feet getting weary as they are yelled at by some earnest and well-intentioned guide, but the deserted city is so huge that they are swallowed up, and one can walk through a landscape with pillars, warm in the sunlight, very much as Dr Halifax had done. There are now no 'Mountain Arabs' to give one the jitters, but there are still large areas of the city unexcavated and often there is the impression that one is walking through one of those delicious, pale, sunny, water-colour landscapes by Pars. It is then that one knows and feels that one is treading in the footprints of history and following Dr Halifax, the redoubtable sea captains Irby and Mangles, Wood and Dawkins, Lady Hester Stanhope who all came and wondered.

* Letters from the Duke of Wellington to the author.

CHAPTER FOUR

'The Pomp of Buildings'

THE mid-eighteenth century saw a serious-minded attempt on the part of architects to study the remains of Classical buildings in Rome, and further afield, as a source of inspiration for their own works. This move back to 'the real thing' is called Neo-Classicism. By no means all architects practising at that time enjoyed the opportunity of travel and research in Italy, but some of those who did go produced immaculately illustrated folios of the 'designs of the antients'. These were intended primarily to introduce themselves to wealthy prospective patrons. Their folios also provided a useful compendium of authentic classical forms and details to which those less fortunate architects and gentlemen could turn for reference—and inspiration.

One can imagine Wood's excitement, therefore, when he and Dawkins first saw the ruins of Palmyra. They had travelled widely seeing ruins by the score, but here at Palmyra was something altogether richer than anything they had experienced before. It is interesting that much of what they selected to illustrate was novel to the established repertoire of the classical vocabulary. Without realising it, they had become aware of some of the factors which set Palmyrene architecture aside from the main-stream of the Syro/Roman tradition; what we today recognise as the 'Parthian Connection'.

The architecture of Palmyra falls within the wide arms of the Hellenistic tradition. The language is the Classical Orders, but expressed in the terms of a virile local tradition. The fact that it was more remotely situated than Baalbeck, Jerash and Apamea, for example, would have helped foster this local character. Prior to the final rebuilding of the Temple of Bel, the structures of the town would have been singularly un-architectural for all their reported monumentality. Mud brick and soft limestone were the main materials, and it is not surprising that precious little of this has survived. It can safely be assumed that there was no early school of architectural style, only a vernacular building tradition based entirely on expertise amassed and handed down over the ages.

All of a sudden the Temple of Bel was erected, an enormous building in a fully mature style, made of hard limestone and demonstrating a technical skill of the first order. Nothing remotely like this had ever been attempted in Palmyra before.

How could the unimportant town of Tadmor even contemplate financing a structure of this size and architectural magnificence, even if they had had the skilled craftsmen to undertake the work. Dr Colledge is probably right in suggesting that Rome under Tiberius was responsible not only for underpinning the finances but also for bringing to Palmyra the masons and stone-carvers to do the work. This can be seen as a political gesture at a time when Rome was not in a position to control the oasis but realised the need to bring its influence to bear.

What is really important is that 'The architecture of the Temple introduced to the growing city a host of forms of eastern Hellenistic type . . .'* During the long building period of the Temple and its Temenos, the Palmyrenes acquired the necessary stylistic knowledge and technical know-how to embark upon buildings of similar style and construction on their own initiative.

Although the first-century architecture of the Temple of Bel is firmly rooted in the Hellenistic tradition, there are some eastern influences at play even at this early date. The ritual layout is Semitic in origin and there are other aspects which establish right from the outset the so-called 'Parthian, involvement in the Palmyrene interpretation which distinguishes their architectural work from the Hellenism of Asia Minor. Nonetheless, the taproot of the style is Hellenism—with strong and influential traces from links with Ptolemaic Egypt.

The north and south walls of the Cella of the Temple of Bel are entirely Greek in inspiration (Fig. 27). Two tall, slender, fluted Ionic half columns, flanked by two square, unfluted corner pilasters, are set against a completely blank surface. The decorative carving is confined to the capitals alone. One almost has the impression of a portico *in antis* which has been walled-up. The carving of the capitals is refined and perfectly in scale. The fluting of the columns of the peristyle surrounding the Cella, which once bore gilded bronze Corinthian capitals, is equally beautiful in its restraint yet with no loss of boldness (Colour Plate 1). The whole composition is calm, predictable and logical—hall-marks of Classical Greek architecture: there is no call here for 'movement' or dramatic effect.

By contrast the west side, which contains the colossal entrance portal, has elements of high drama which one comes to expect from the inventive nature of eastern Hellenism. This drama is concentrated in the portal itself which was structurally incorporated into the peristyle. It provided an emphatic break in the rhythm of the colonnade and emphasised the importance of the doorway itself. In its design the influence of Ptolemaic Egypt is strongly felt (see page 118). The interruption of rhythm, the emphatic gesture and the change of planes, all create a sense of controlled 'movement' which is almost baroque in character (Figs. 59 and 57). Robert Adam, in the eighteenth century, was to describe 'movement' as 'the

* *The Art of Palmyra.*

78

Fig. 27 The south wall of the Temple of Bel.

rise and fall, the advance and recess, with other diversity of form, in the different parts of a building, so as to add greatly to the picturesqueness of the composition ...' The prominence of the doorway is heightened by a far more profuse use of carving round the architrave and scroll corbels which supported an equally lavishly decorated subsidiary entablature (now badly eroded). It was the development of the sense of 'movement' and the variety and richness of decoration that revealed the most evident characteristics of the local tradition.

The sculptural decoration of the twenty-ton beams which held the columns of the peristyle to the Cella walls, and which carried the carved ceiling, demonstrate the presence of the eastern influence (Fig. 8). Above a base of richly carved, very Hellenistic, vine scroll and a band of egg and dart moulding there is a panel of figurative relief which is distinctly 'Parthian'. The juxtaposition of schemes such as this was a marked Palmyrene trait. It is much more evident in portrait sculpture

Fig. 28 A selection of the 'complicated geometric' designs copied and published in *The Ruins of Palmyra*.

than in architectural form, but flat surface decoration, with its lack of undercutting and complicated geometric designs (Figs. 28 and 38), hints at these influences.

There is an almost oriental splendour about the later works in Palmyra which makes one feel the deep-lying eastern influence. Florid richness of decorative carving, heightened by vivid colouring, spreads profusely over everything. Indeed Palmyra in its heyday must have been one of the most sumptuously decorated cities in the ancient world. Nowhere was the Hellenistic tradition so gorgeously dressed, so brilliantly coloured and so uninhibitedly enjoyed.

This uninhibited enjoyment of controlled elaboration was often expressed in some inventive and original designs, particularly in the context of town planning, where new spatial relationships were explored. These local architectural ideas and achievements in town planning never seem to have influenced other sites or cities. The reverse is also true, the development of Palmyrene architecture does not appear to have been stimulated and refreshed by contact with other Syrian towns. That Palmyra was able to develop along her own local lines resulted in some very singular, individual interpretations of late Hellenistic architectural thought and practice.

The town planning of the city is worth considering for it not only provided a marvellous vehicle for their grand civic constructions but it is interesting on its own account.

It was a Greek, Hippodamus of Miletus, who made the 'revolutionary discovery—or so it seemed, just as it was to seem again in the twentieth century—namely that it is possible, and even desirable, to P L A N towns, not just let them sprawl . . .'* Not that all subsequent Hellenistic cities were laid out on the Hippodamian grid system, like Priene, but the effects to be achieved by laying out a site to the best visual as well as practical advantage were increasingly appreciated. At Pergamon, where there is no suggestion of a grid, the slope of the site is used to great theatrical effect. Many other cities likewise planned their important ceremonial sectors with an eye to gaining the maximum dramatic effect.

It is this dramatic effect that is so strikingly displayed at Palmyra. The developments of the second and third centuries were to create a series of townscapes and monuments which had all the illusionist architectonics of a Bibbiena stage set. Probably the most noticeable feature of this was the creation of the Colonnade Street (Map 4). Such porticoed avenues were by no means uncommon in Roman Syria of this time—there are fine ones at Jerash and Apamea, and another at Petra—but in Palmyra the whole scheme was carried out on such a colossal scale and was so sumptuously ornamented that it stands as a particularly splendid example. There is so much of it left even today that the city can justly be considered one of the most spectacular survivals of this kind of civic development. A street which previously had been a mere means of communication, probably an uninviting dust-track between the plain, uninteresting walls of inward-looking buildings, was now transformed into a monumental feature of the city in its own right. Along it lay important structures whose entrances were architecturally integrated into the overall design.

Long vistas down streets need some large-scale feature to terminate the view, something at the end to catch the eye and resolve the composition. Much the same happened in seventeenth- and eighteenth-century Europe, not only in townscapes but in the great tree-lined avenues across a nobleman's park finishing up with a towering column, obelisk, folly or arch.

* Stewart Perone, *Geographical Magazine*, Vol. 37, 1964.

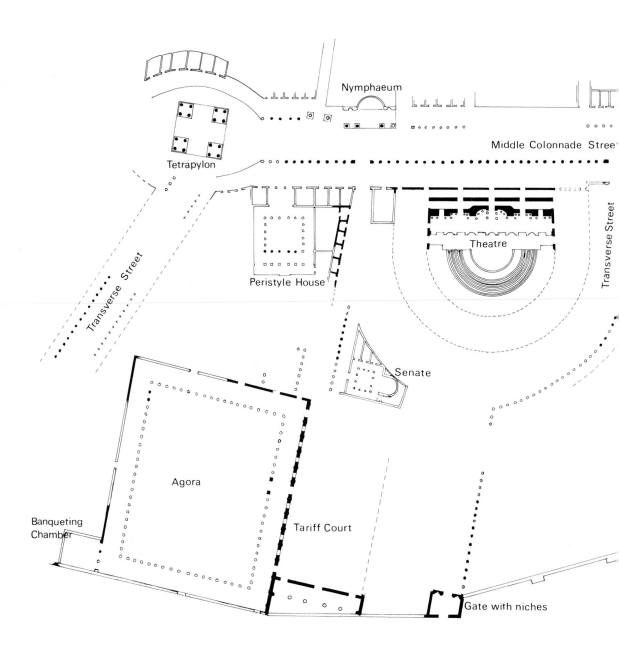

Map 4 Plan of the civic centre of Palmyra.

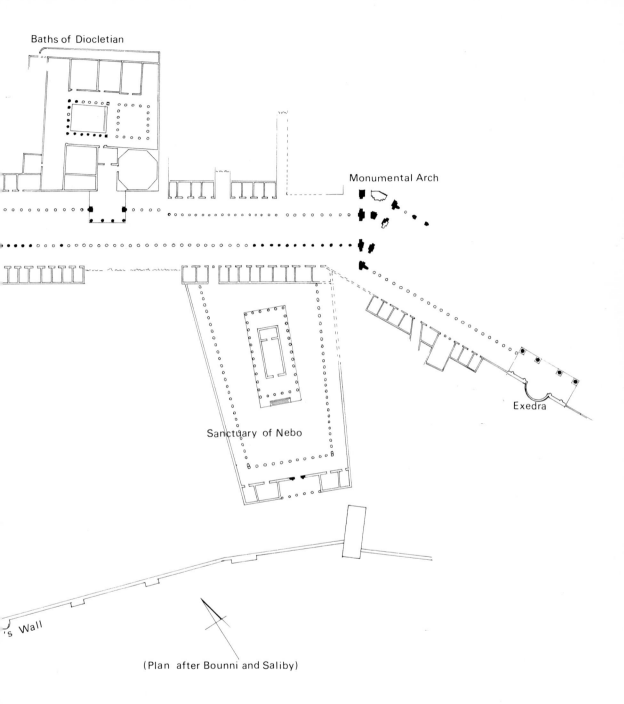

Baths of Diocletian

Monumental Arch

Exedra

Sanctuary of Nebo

's Wall

(Plan after Bounni and Saliby)

Judging from the dates on the inscriptions on the pillars carrying brackets, the first leg of the street to have been aggrandised was the section running from the Funerary Temple down to the Tetrapylon. The western end was terminated by the Temple itself, the façade being exactly aligned on the Colonnade Street (Fig. 29). A fine effect was achieved by having the portico of the Temple seen through an arch (now vanished) which was set a few steps up from pavement level (Fig. 117). A feeling of space was thus created which drew the viewer through the arch and so out of the confines of the street into a spacious 'piazza' dominated by the portico of the Temple. This is pure axial planning handled with an alert sense of the dramatic.

The areas on either side of this western leg of the street are laid out with clearly defined streets and the insubstantial remains of many prosperous houses in the various *insulae*. These areas were probably redeveloped at about the same time as the Colonnade Street.

The Colonnade Street is also aligned exactly on the Temple of Bel far away to the east, and the original intention may have been to cut it right through the existing town in one long, straight thoroughfare. Had this been done we would have had the longest street in the ancient world, but it would have involved the total destruction of the Temple of Nebo, an ancient and much venerated site, besides much else of civic importance. The solution was to change the direction of the street a few degrees to the north thus narrowly avoiding the Nebo Sanctuary and the main concentration of civic buildings.

This change of direction created an awkward visual problem at the eastern end of the first leg. The architecturally weak oblique view of the colonnade of the next section needed to be masked by a strong feature without obstructing the flow of traffic. The problem was further complicated by the intersection of two other streets at this point.

The result was the monumental Tetrapylon set in a roughly oval 'piazza'. The Tetrapylon serves no practical purpose and is purely decorative. For all its monumentality it is a light and airy conception and one has exciting views through it to the forest of columns which line the next, middle, leg of the street. As with the arch of the Funerary Temple, a sense of depth and 'space beyond' is created. Seen from the middle leg it is particularly impressive (Fig. 30) because one looks up a slight rise with it towering imposingly above one.

The middle section of the Street has three features which are important in terms of monumental townscape. The arches which admit intersecting streets, the forward projecting portico of the Baths of Diocletian, and the Monumental Arch.

The colonnade on the south side is interrupted to accommodate two intersecting streets. The rhythm is momentarily broken by a wide archway whilst the momentum is maintained by the entablature which runs unimpeded. These arches are

Fig. 29 The Funerary Temple and the
Upper Colonnade Street.

Fig. 30 The reconstructed Tetrapylon.

Fig. 31 Reconstruction of the intersection of a side street with the main Colonnade Street.

Fig. 32 Reconstruction of the Colonnade Street looking towards the Monumental Arch.

repeated behind in the rear wall of the covered portico. Today the effect is lost but originally one would have had a view from the sunlit street through a wide arch into the shade of the colonnade, through another arch and so into the sunlight again of another street whose columns are seen at right angles (Fig. 31). A practical arrangement that is most theatrical and displays an appreciation of the play of light and shade in architectural composition.

This awareness of the dramatic quality of chiaroscuro—the interplay of light and shade—is very much a baroque phenomenon and was one fully understood by the Palmyrene designers. Apart from the practical value of colonnades in providing shade, they create rich patterns of light and shade.

Rhythm is also important in architecture. Had the colonnade run from the Tetrapylon to the Monumental Arch in an unbroken sequence of pillars it would have been less interesting. As it is, the two intersection archways break the pillared façade into three sections and so give a 'beat' to the steady rhythm of evenly spaced pillars.

The portico of the Baths of Diocletian (Fig. 81) stands forward slightly of the main street façade and so, like the arches opposite, breaks the monotony of a long, unrelieved run of pillars. The portico was also higher than the colonnades, thus

creating a very emphatic punctuation mark in the design. The portico was also emphasised by its pillars being of dull red granite whereas everything else was of pale honey-coloured hard limestone which is such a co-ordinating factor in the ruins today.

The colonnades of the street must, however, be considered together and not as separate concepts. They are both parts of the same design. Today this is by no means easy to grasp because so much of the northern colonnade is lost and one is only conscious of the southern. It was this which trapped Dr Halifax into believing that the south colonnade was the pillared façade of a palace. When both sides were standing (Fig. 32) it was far from being two unrelated colonnades enclosing the street. The breaks in the rhythm created by the intersection arches and the projection of the portico of the Baths of Diocletian, so punctuated the design that the street was full of architectural variety and interest. Add to this the richness of the carved detail, the vivid colouring of painted sculpture and the multitude of statues which stood on the brackets, and one has one of the most exciting and dramatic streets to have come down to us from the ancient world.

Architectural excitement and ingenuity allied to sumptuously carved ornament reached a peak in the Monumental Arch which terminates the middle leg of the

street at its eastern end (Fig. 32). This Arch concealed another bend which turns the street back again in the direction of the Temple of Bel. The change in direction is rather more than at the Tetrapylon, in this case 30°, so an imposing feature was most certainly needed to terminate the vista.

The monument can be dated approximately to the end of the second century when Palmyrene architecture was assuming its most developed and florid form.

The plan of the Arch (Fig. 70) is trapezoidal—or 'V' shaped—so that both the main façades are squarely aligned to each section of the street. Variety was achieved in this double composition by the façade facing up the middle section of the street engaging the colonnades on either side of the tall central arch, whereas the façade on the other side, which faces up to the Temple of Bel, engages them on either side of the full width of the triple arch design (Fig. 33). Having come down the street from the Tetrapylon one would have entered the shade of the central archway without being able to see the vista up the final section to the Temple. Having been architecturally guided round 30° one would have emerged and found oneself suddenly in a much wider and infinitely more spacious avenue with the

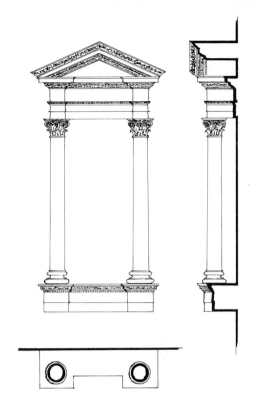

Fig. 33 Reconstruction of the Monumental Arch from the south side.

Fig. 34 Architectural composition known as a 'Syrian' niche.

colossal Propylaea of the Temple riding hugely at anchor ahead of one. The dramatic impact of this was superbly contrived.

Marvellous though the planning and design of this Arch are, it is the carved ornament which is unmistakably Palmyrene. It encrusts with the greatest richness the niches which were crowned with broken pediments (known as Syrian pediments): the hoods of the arches are elaborately enriched (Fig. 34) with an eclectic combination of lotus leaves, egg and dart moulding and foliated straps, whilst the pilaster panels contain stylised floral and leaf carvings of bewildering variety (Fig. 72). It is the soffits of the side arches, however, which display that most Palmyrene decorative characteristic, their love of complicated geometric design (Figs. 28 and 38). No two soffits are the same; gone are the rigid coffers of Roman art, and in their place is an amazing counter-play of curves and straight lines. This lush variety within the strict confines of a clearly articulated order gives the Arch a peculiarly oriental splendour.

Palmyrene ornamental carving was florid—but this appealed to the temperament of the people who used it unashamedly whenever and wherever possible. But the ornament was always well controlled and never sought to assert itself at the expense of the overall design.

During their two week stay in the ruins Wood and Dawkins were not only struck by the virtuosity of much of the architectural design—particularly the Arch and the

Fig. 35 Gavin Hamilton's painting of Wood and Dawkins
discovering Palmyra, painted in 1758.

Temple of Bel—but also by the variety and originality of the ornament. They
copied many examples of the geometric design to which they devoted whole plates
(Fig. 28). Clearly they realised that the classical language had developed here far
along local, individual lines. The seminal structure of the Temple of Bel was still
there but the style it had introduced had developed into something which was
entirely new. They had discovered a wealth of 'new' classical details which would
be of 'some advantage to the publick'.

They returned to England and, in 1753, published the volumes which were to
make them famous.

The Ruins of Palmyra otherwise Tedmor in the Desert provided a great stimulus to
designers, and the ruins, via Wood and Dawkins, became the source of much
architectural and artistic inspiration. The publication gave impetus to the Neo-
Classical movement, a fact recognised in 1758 by the Scottish Neo-Classical
painter, Gavin Hamilton, in his dual portrait of the two travellers entitled *The*

Discovery of Palmyra by Wood and Dawkins (Fig. 35). The two gentlemen, swathed in Roman togas and surrounded by a posse of Arab guides and camels, gesticulate down the Colonnade Street towards the Monumental Arch. Despite the absurdity and improbability of the scene portrayed it is a unique instance of an artist paying tribute to the two men who had done so much to forward the Neo-Classical Age of which he was a prominent member.

The short and intuitive period of the Baroque, which used the Classical Orders with little regard for the Vitruvian canon, was over in Britain and men of taste and learning were looking back to Rome for points of reference and precedents. Lord Burlington had revived Palladio whose rules were based on those of the ancient Roman architect Vitruvius. Inigo Jones had done the same before, but his efforts had been cut short by the Commonwealth. But by 1753 Palladianism was becoming outmoded, and architects were foraging amongst the ruins of the Roman past for a more correct, more authentic classical style.

Most country houses had in their libraries a copy of *The Ruins* and this was referred to avidly. The results were not always wholly satisfactory, for sometimes the designer did not fully grasp the style he was handling. A charming example of this is at Grey's Court, near Henley-on-Thames, where an upstairs room is referred to, even in today's National Trust Guide, as having a Palmyra ceiling. In fact the ceiling is not remotely Palmyrene but the deep plaster frieze which runs round the room proudly boasts some stocky eagles with wings outspread that can be traced directly to Plate XVIII in *The Ruins*. The squire of the day felt he had up-dated the decoration by incorporating a feature from the Temple of Bel (termed the Temple of the Sun in *The Ruins*). There are many recorded examples of this kind of thing and probably many more unrecognised and unrecorded elsewhere in the country.

The professionals also latched onto *The Ruins*, for as early as 1753, the year of publication, Thomas Clayton, the stuccoist, submitted a bill for work at Blair Castle in Scotland, in which he charged for a 'Palmyra ceiling' and a 'Palmyra cornice'. The Front Stairs at Blair Castle, which can be dated to 1757, also has a ceiling in which one sees the influence of *The Ruins*. In 1754–9, the Adam Brothers created the Drawing Room at Dumfries House, Ayrshire, which has a ceiling of free octagons round a central circular motif contained in a rectangle that recalls Plate XIX—a Plate which was a decade later to become the inspiration for Robert Adam's famous Palmyra ceiling at Osterley Park House in Middlesex. Adam drew on the spirit of *The Ruins* again when he created, between 1761–6, the ceiling in the Gallery at Croome Court, Worcestershire. Although the basic design of the coffering is derived from the Basilica of Constantine, there are strong affinities to Plate VIII in the way details are handled and in the rich interplay of octagons and smaller squares.

Two examples of ceilings which are unmistakably Palmyrene, and over which there can be no argument as to the source of inspiration, are at Stratfield Saye House near Reading, Berkshire. In the Dining Room (Fig. 36), added by George Pitt around 1775, the ceiling is directly inspired by Plate XIX. This is the Plate which shows the ceilings of the north and south adytons of the Temple of Bel (see pages 122 and 124). The design of the ceiling is based on that in the south adyton but is very much thinned out and attenuated to a point of becoming spidery. The broad circle of meander is pared down to a slim shadow of the original, and the central motif is drastically reduced. The original in Palmyra has enormous guts emphasised by the depth of its carving. The Stratfield Saye ceiling is very flat and has none of the structural look of the original (the Palmyra ceiling is in fact a monolith and is in no way structural, but this is not the point). The Dining Room ceiling is, however, an elegant performance which accords well with the more precise and refined tastes of eighteenth-century England as opposed to the agressive opulence of ancient Palmyra. The designer caught well, and in some respects emphasised by his starving the design, the interplay of geometric shapes so beloved of the Palmyrenes.

The Library at Stratfield Saye also has a 'Palmyra' ceiling, this time inspired by a detail in Plate VIII. Again it catches the overall geometric patterning of Palmyrene designs. In both cases the decoration was applied on the flat surface of the ceiling rather than sunk into the plaster as coffers: the material used was probably papier maché.

It is surprising that Giovanni Battistia Borra, who made all the drawings for the publication, should have refrained from indulging his researches when he was architect at Stowe House in Buckinghamshire. In all the work he did there, there is nothing which one can say with conviction is directly inspired by *The Ruins*. There is a wealth of classical detail from his hand but it is mostly of a type he could have found anywhere in the Roman world.

The most important single work inspired directly by *The Ruins* is Robert Adam's ceiling in the Drawing Room at Osterley Park House, the room which Walpole described as 'the drawing room worthy of Eve before the Fall'. Adam had done site drawings himself at Diocletian's Palace at Split in Yugoslavia, and probably because of this he appreciated how a drawing should be best interpreted.

The main difference between the design of the Osterley ceiling (Fig. 37) and Plate XIX (Fig. 38) is that Adam substitutes an oval for the circular central feature. This was done to make the design fit into an oblong room. Adam also added an extra row of octagons at each end and substituted a two tier plume motif in place of the rather stiff circle of little feathers radiating from a sunflower which shows in the Wood and Dawkins drawing. The drawing was, however, inaccurate for the original ceiling in Palmyra has alternating lotus and acanthus within the

Fig. 36 The Dining Room ceiling at Stratfield Saye House, based on that of the south adyton of the Temple of Bel.

Fig. 37 The finest eighteenth-century adaptation of the south adyton ceiling design, the Drawing Room ceiling at Osterley Park House by Robert Adam.

Fig. 38 The design of the ceiling in the south adyton of the Temple of Bel as depicted in *The Ruins of Palmyra* by Wood and Dawkins.

central broad band of meander. The coffering at Osterley is not nearly so pronounced as in Palmyra but it avoids looking weak and stringy. Its flatter relief is certainly more appropriate to an English drawing room than the bold musculature of the original. The number of octagons (seventy-two) round the central feature is also reduced making the size of each larger in proportion. This in turn meant that the tight rosettes which fill the coffers in Palmyra are at Osterley grown into large open, swirling blooms. It is amazing what a change of climate will do. As a result of substituting an oval for a circle and cutting the depth of the relief, Adam was presented with the necessity of filling the four spandrels round the oval with rather more elaborate decorative motifs. If anything is out of keeping in this design it is the rococo squirls which he used. Wood and Dawkins's spandrel decorations in Plate XIX were only small paterae as exist in the original (Fig. 64) so Adam can perhaps be excused. The geometric patterning is well caught and the whole ensemble is a magnificent and fitting ceiling for a stately drawing room. Adam's design is sophisticated, thoroughly English Neo-Classical, and polite. It is not surprising, therefore, that the tension, depth and 'structural' rigidity of the original has been lost. Refinement there is in both, but in one it is the refinement of social manners, in the other, the refinement of western asiatic religious fervour.

Throughout his career, Adam relied to a considerable extent on *The Ruins* even though he produced a similar volume to *The Ruins* with his own publication on Diocletian's Palace at Spalato (Split). This work not only enhanced his reputation but also gave him a further storehouse of inspiration. But it is interesting that, as Sir John Summerson has pointed out, 'Spalato . . . provided him with less material than, for instance, Robert Wood's Palmyra and Baalbeck folios or Le Roy's description of the ruins of Greece . . .'* Other works by him identified as deriving from Palmyra can be recorded at Bowood, Compton Verney and Audley End.

Adam, however, was not alone in using *The Ruins* as a source of inspiration, for others also turned to the Plates in their search for details. The plasterer William Rhodes, made the ceiling of the Salon at Drayton House, Northamptonshire in 1771. He was a craftsman with a noteworthy list of achievements but the intricacies of Plate XIX were evidently beyond him as a designer. Not only is the relief too shallow but the scale of the individual components of the design is too small. In consequence there is an absolute spate of octagons (one hundred and thirty-five as opposed to seventy-two at Osterley). The central circle of meander containing an emasculated feather motif, is so small that it hardly makes any impression. The overall effect is fussy with too many surrounding octagons competing for attention with too small a central feature. The design remains unresolved. Adam did not make this mistake: at Osterley he expanded the central circle into an oval which dominated the composition and reduced the octagons to a subordinate and supporting role.

The Hall at West Wycombe Park in Buckinghamshire also has a ceiling based on Plate XIX. In this case an Italian artist was employed to paint the design on the ceiling. Not surprisingly the result looks flat and has little architectural impact. The complicated geometry of the designs published in *The Ruins* when applied to ceilings, depends on relief. Other rooms in the house have doorcases, cornices etc., painted with a wide selection of architectural decorative details extracted from *The Ruins*.

At Milton Abbas in Dorset, Joseph Rose, the master plasterer, created the Library ceiling in 1775. Of all the ceilings derived from Plate XIX it is probably the one which most faithfully reflects, detail for detail, Borra's original drawing. The fact is very evident that here we have a fine craftsman working unguided by an

* *Architecture in Britain, 1530–1830.*

accomplished architect (even though James Wyatt was working on the house at this time, there is no evidence to suggest that he designed the ceiling). The standard of the plasterwork is exceptionally high, as one would expect from Rose, and the handling of the design is assured; his long working association with Adam might account for this. But it is no longer a question of influence or interpretation and, in consequence, the ceiling lacks the same excitement which one feels when considering the subtleties of adaptation to be seen in Adam's drawing room at Osterley.

It is interesting to note that, of all the designs which appeared in *The Ruins*, it is Plate XIX which seems to have been drawn upon most. It is not possible to account for this for there are other designs which are of equal beauty and which might well have provided equal potential.

A few antagonists disapproved of Palmyrene architecture as revealed in *The Ruins*, such as James Paine who never shed his Palladianism for all the Neo-Classical details he frequently used in his later works. He was not far from the mark, however, when he wrote '... although Palmyra and Baalbeck are curious works, they furnish no new light in the great parts of architecture, and are only valuable for the ornament'. His attitude is well demonstrated in his own works where one has a basically Palladian structure with refined Neo-Classical detailing. Sir William Chambers, Adam's most powerful rival and critic, stuck to his cool, elegant classicism in which 'the great parts of architecture' are clearly and boldly stated, and only used Neo-Classical detail and decoration when it served the desired architectural end. However, in his *Treatise on Civil Architecture*, a work of considerable merit and for long a textbook for architectural students, he drew on *The Ruins* and in the plates showing designs for coved ceilings, he copied several of the geometric patterns which Wood and Dawkins had recorded.

It is not intended here to give a list of all the works which were inspired by *The Ruins* even if that were possible. Those examples already discussed will give some indication of the extent and type of work which relied on the publication. It should also be pointed out that the influence extended far beyond providing 'material'—beyond directly copying a design or making a not very distant variation on it. The folio influenced the whole concept of architectural design and decoration. Its main effect was on ornament, and much of the richness and variety of Neo-Classical decoration finds its roots in an awareness brought home— literally and metaphorically—by Wood and Dawkins. Thus a Neo-Classicism developed in British architecture which was at once richly ornamented with classical motifs 'borrowed' from the past, refined and sophisticated. Nonetheless, the work was also influential in that it broadened the general classical horizon.

Eventually, of course, the building public tired and sought even more classical sources, turning to James (Athenian) Stuart and Nicholas Revett who had published their measured drawings of Athens in 1762. So was the pace of the Greek Revival set. The publication notice of Sayer's folio, *The Ruins of Athens*, maintained that the Greek Revival was an 'attempt to restore architecture to its ancient dignity'. In another respect it was the war cry of the Greeks versus the Romans in the battle of styles which was thereafter to rage in the corridors of classical architecture.

The continent of Europe did not go through the Palladian upheaval which dominated British architecture; indeed there seems to have been a much greater degree of continuity in stylistic development without the early resort to revival movements which both beset and enriched English architecture. France stuck to her own stylistic sources, developing early a classicism very much her own. This is to be seen in the works of Mansard and Le Vaux who consciously referred to Roman works for precedents. But their style might be termed 'Louis-Classicism' rather than Neo-Classicism, into which it gradually evolved. By the time the Neo-Classical Movement swept across Europe with the Greek Revival hot on its heels Boullée and Ledoux had already discovered that the severity and heaviness of ancient buildings was diametrically opposed to the tempered taste of classicism. The revelation of lightness and gaiety in such publications as *The Ruins* lies behind many of Boullée's designs.

The impact of *The Ruins* was also felt in eastern Europe and Russia. In the works of Cameron it is particularly evident. His Neo-Classicism is a refreshing mixture of stylistic refinement and 'the great parts of architecture'.

In America the story is altogether different. The so-called 'Colonial' style was developed in New England at the time when Palladianism was changing the face of English building. Much of the earliest colonial work leant heavily on the William and Mary cum Anne vernacular, but the later impact of Palladianism was revolutionary. Duly adapted and interpreted it became the fundamental driving force in Eastern seaboard America. The list of fine buildings which looked to Palladio via Burlington is still considerable. The States were essentially conservative and, having evolved a style which suited them, they did not like to change. It is not surprising, therefore, that the lush, Graeco-Roman and Hellenistic styles of Palmyra should have fallen on deaf ears.

The architecture in Palmyra was something very different from what appeared under that name in the drawing rooms of England. It 'reflected the ways of thinking, the trends and interests of their own society'.* That society was, despite the Hellenistic guise it adopted in its architecture, basically eastern, and the underlying, constant, theme of its art was Near Eastern. Architecture for the Palmyrenes was one way of expressing their ideas, their racial identity and their enjoyment of life.

* *The Art of Palmyra.*

1 The peristyle of the Temple of Bel
(*see* p. 116)

2 Ain Efqa (*see* p. 204)

3 Fallen fluted columns in the Temenos
of the Sanctuary of Bel (*see* p. 128)

CHAPTER FIVE

Palmyra Today

FROM the busy, leafy town of Homs the road to Palmyra drives eastwards between red fields with bright patches of green all round, and prosperous whitewashed farmhouses dotting the landscape. Soon these rich, undulating farmlands give way to the buff colouring of the desert, which in spring is softened with the gentle green of grasses and shrubs, and a profusion of gaily coloured wild flowers. As though to take you unawares, low hills slowly close in to the north and south until you are progressing along a wide valley with swelling highlands to left and to right. There is an air of busy silence; crops await the sickle, cattle, sheep and goats stand aimlessly in the sun or move forward judiciously step by step, devouring each delicious blade of grass.

After about an hour a range of hills across the valley seems to herald the end of the journey. The flat valley now starts to undulate and make the road slip and curve round the shallow contours, affording a glimpse of a castle perched on the top of the centre hill. The 'Bride of the Desert' cannot be all that far off.

Round a bold left hand corner one suddenly looks down on a spectacular array of pillars and walls basking in the sunshine. This first distant view of the city is unforgettable. Never more so than on one's first visit when the surprise is so marvellous. It is best seen in the evening as the sun is going down and the enclosing hills are already sunk in darkness, leaving the city bathed in golden light against a darkening indigo sky.

It was a view well known to ancient travellers as they approached along the old Damascus road—now the Valley of Tombs. The surviving ruins are seen here from such an angle that they form one composition, spread across the floor of the plain below and yet contained by the girdle of dark green trees of the oasis.

As you approach out of the hills they seem to disperse and arrange themselves into famous groups.

The site of the ancient city covers a vast area. Much still remains to be excavated, and often one has the impression of wandering through an eighteenth-century print with broken colonnades and walls rising silently from the ground, unattended and unrestored. Narrow tracks wind their aimless way through desert grasses and succulents which cover the ground, without the ordered purpose of

◀ **4** (*Above*) Gebel Umm el Belquis at the entry to the Valley of Tombs (*see* p. 193); (*below*) The Funerary Temple (*see* p. 176) and the Tower Tombs on Umm el Belquis from one of the ruined peristyles (*see* p. 170)

science. The ruins present moments of great drama and of beguiling gentleness, and yet there is always that ebbing sense of space with distant views, hazy blue and silver, through a colonnade and out past a time-scarred wall.

The exploration of the ruins which follows is divided into zones, which will provide a continuous 'walk-round' text for those who need it but which will also serve those who seek information on selected areas.

Fig. 39 The remains of some patrician houses to the south of the Sanctuary of Bel.

PALMYRA TODAY

Patrician Houses, the Sanctuary of Bel and Eastern Colonnade Street

The Sanctuary of Bel is the largest and most important single ruin remaining in Palmyra. Before considering this massive monument, however, attention should be given to a small excavation immediately to the east of the Temenos wall. It is of two PATRICIAN HOUSES dating from the third century A.D., which were excavated by Duru in 1940. These were buildings of considerable extent and certainly of handsome character comparable in scale and stateliness with those in Zone Three (see page 170). A couple of pillared courtyards with peristyles are clearly visible, as are many of the rooms off them (Fig. 39). The smaller of these apartments probably belonged to the women of the family.

The importance of these houses lies in their fine mosaics, now in the Palmyra and Damascus museums. The colouring is rich, with the closely grouped composition still permitting a considerable amount of movement and fluidity of line. Two depict scenes taken from the Trojan Wars as related by the Roman poet Statius, presumably from material now lost to us. Achilles was educated by the Centaur, Chiron, and Odysseus finds him on the island of Scyros where he has been hidden by his father Peleus, King of Thessaly. The first scene depicts Achilles and Odysseus together, whilst the second is of a centaur—perhaps Chiron. Both mosaics came from the so-called 'women's apartments' and are much damaged. The third is very fine and depicts the legend of Cassiopeia, wife of Cepheus, King of Ethiopia, and mother of Andromeda. It was she who rashly boasted that her daughter was more beautiful than the Nereids, thus incurring the anger of Poseidon. To show his displeasure he sent a sea monster to ravage her lands, only to be placated by the sacrifice of the innocent Andromeda. This mosaic was removed to Damascus Museum, except for a fragment which has been kept in the Palmyra Museum.

Amongst other 'finds' in these excavations was a collection of statuettes made of plaster which is also in the Palmyra Museum.

The SANCTUARY OF BEL (Fig. 40) still looms proud and monumental, its sheer bulk providing a much needed visual anchor to the eastern end of the city. A vast Temenos enclosed the Temple proper, and to gain a true impression of its size it is worth walking round the outside of the massive walls. It has the appearance of Graeco-Roman work, but the plan (Fig. 41) of the Temple itself is Syrian.

The north-western corner, towards which one normally approaches the monument today, is well preserved. The internal colonnades behind these walls were the same height on the northern, eastern and southern sides but the western, which housed the Propylaea, was raised higher, and the junction in levels is clearly seen

Fig. 40 The Sanctuary of Bel.

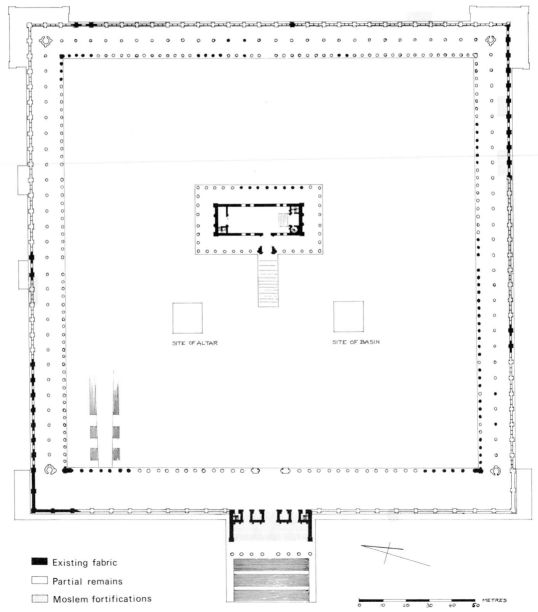

SITE OF ALTAR

SITE OF BASIN

■ Existing fabric

☐ Partial remains

▨ Moslem fortifications

METRES
0   10   20   30   40   50

Fig. 41 The plan of the Sanctuary of Bel.

Fig. 42 The north-west corner of the Temenos wall.

at this corner. Nonetheless, they were all treated in the same manner with Corinthian pilasters standing on a high podium and carrying a fully articulated entablature: between each pilaster was a framed window topped by a triangular pediment. Only seven and a half bays now remain of the north wall, the remainder having collapsed. This was rebuilt, with no pretentions to architecture, when the Sanctuary was fortified during the Seljuk period. However, one can still imagine what the wall would have looked like in its original state (Fig. 42).

101

Fig. 43 Part of the east wall which was rebuilt from fallen masonry with carved details such as pediments and pilaster capitals reused at random and with no heed to their original architectural relationships.

Fig. 44 The south wall of the ▶ Sanctuary of Bel.

The east wall has a fascination of its own owing to the manner in which many of the collapsed parts were reinstated. A short first section is of rubble construction but it soon gives way to a fragment on which there are clear traces of pilasters and niches. Then comes a long section of non-architectural wall of re-used original material. The blocks have been relaid on their sides so that the securing groove is exposed. Yet more curious is the almost random inclusion of pairs of pilaster capitals and irregularly placed window pediments. Their positioning has nothing to do with the original architectural pattern; nor are they all placed at a consistent height (Fig. 43). All the dressed stones of this fallen section must have been lying on the ground and were used as they came to hand in the reconstruction.

Beyond this point there are two short sections of rubble wall wedging a solitary pilaster, with entablature and all, which has keeled over backwards at a most drunken angle. The south-east corner is dominated by a tall tower with a machiolated parapet of re-used dressed stones. This is part of the Islamic fortifications. A heavily buttressed stretch of rubble wall then turns the corner to the south wall.

The south wall retains substantial sections of the original (Fig. 44) but these have had to be stabilised by powerful concrete beams along their bases. The very real danger that the foundations might fail and send the whole lot crashing down into the wooded valley below is evident from the alarming backwards lean of the middle part. This is now stoutly supported on the inside by massive buttresses. Beyond this point there is another late Islamic rebuilding using old masonry, then another fragment of the original wall and finally a long run of rubble work.

On the west the rubble wall gives immediately onto another tall Islamic tower, the face of which projects slightly forward of the original line of the wall. To its left is a thick semi-circular bastion made of sections of Roman pillars laid side by side (right hand side of Fig. 45). Over this short section loom six of the monumental pillars remaining from the huge internal peristyle.

Beyond a modern gate into the Temenos stand the remains of the colossal PROPYLAEA. This was converted into the citadel when the whole Sanctuary was fortified by Abdul Hassan Yussuf ibn Fairouz in 1132–3 and therefore is more of a

103

fortress than a grandiose entrance to the Sacred Temenos. Grandiose, however, it was in antiquity. All that remains visible of the original western elevation are the two flanking walls, each terminating in a Corinthian pilaster (Fig. 45). Between these Fairouz built a wall, re-using existing material, with the dressed blocks again being laid sideways so that the securing grooves are exposed. In the middle of this—actually it is well off centre—there projects a tower in which the principal feature is a deeply recessed arch. Above this beautiful curve and counter-curve there is a bracketed machiolation flanked by two pieces of antique carving, probably part of the frieze of the vanished Propylaea. The carving is still crisp, and the figures, Hercules with his club to the right and Mercury with his purse to the left, appear remarkably Bacchanalian for a strict Muslim. They add a delightfully decorative touch to an otherwise very severe façade. Other fragments of carving can be seen high up amongst the flat stones of the towering walls. They are placed at random and no consideration was given to their location. Two pieces of carved string-course wedged between two fragments of geometric fret stand out particularly to the right of the arch. Above the low doorway is an inscription in Florid Cufic script, which records the erection of this bastion.

> In the name of God, the compassionate, the merciful, the building of this wall—may it remain standing—and of the western wall, has been ordered by the Emir, the most distinguished chamberlain, the lord, the great one, with the help of God, Nassir ad-Din, the resource of Islam, the sword, the trust of the Empire, the auxiliary of the defender of faith, the honour of Emirs, the holder of the two nobilities, Abdul-Hassan Yussuf ibn Fairouz, the atabki, of the prince of the believers, at his own expense, in the months of the year 527AH (1132–33).

This powerful structure gives little hint of what it replaces. It is quite likely that the great pillared portico of the Propylaea had collapsed, leaving a deep three-sided cavity which would have been an irresistible invitation to Fairouz to add a fourth wall and thus achieve, with the minimum of building, a 'keep' for the fortified Temenos. This fourth wall is not tied into the flanking classical pilasters which now tend to lean outwards. To prevent any further tilting strong concrete footings have been added.

Unfortunately there is now no trace of the original appearance of the western façade of the Propylaea which was swept away in 1132. A Monumental flight of steps, 35 metres wide, flanked by high plinths, led up to a huge eight-pillared portico which was thrown forward of the two existing corner pilasters. Over the central bay, which was wider than the rest, was a low-pitched arch springing from above the cornice of the flanking entablatures, the whole composition being surmounted by a boldly modelled pediment (Fig. 46).

Fig. 45 The Moslem citadel built on the site of the ancient Propylaea.

Fig. 46 Reconstruction of the Propylaea of the Sanctuary of Bel.

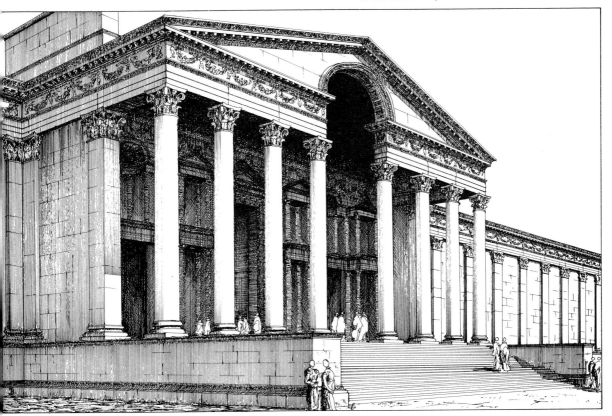

Fig. 47 An 'Assyrian' merlon reconstructed in the Temenos.

Fig. 48 Reconstruction of under the portico of the Propylaea showing the three entrance gates to the Temenos

Much has been written on the Assyrian-like crow-step parapet which some believe lined the tops of all the walls and towers. The strength of the Oriental tradition in Palmyra must be readily admitted but this feature is hard to accept. The archaeological evidence does not amount to very much. The existence of a reconstruction of such a merlon in the Temenos seems scanty premise upon which to postulate that the whole complex was so adorned. The merlon bears more the appearance of an Oriental Palmyrene version of the classical acroteria (Fig. 47). The reconstructions here presented show this feature as acroteria only and are, therefore, at variance with the model of the Sanctuary in the Museum.

Two staircases ascended within the Propylaea and would have come out at roof level in the attic storey which backed the pediment on both façades.

Within the portico, the visitor in antiquity would have been faced with an elaborate screen of pillars and niches across the entrance wall (Fig. 48). This screen was divided into two halves by the colossal doorway; each housing a lower flanking door. The architectural counterpoint was rich and complex with a wealth of the carved detail so beloved of the Palmyrenes. Comparisons can be drawn with the Propylaea of the Temple of Artemis at Jerash, of Jupiter at Baalbeck, and at other great Hellenistic sites in the Levant and its hinterland. Nowhere, however, was the effect of richness and opulence surpassed. On the west face of the east wall, within Fairouz's 'keep', there are still vestiges of this arrangement but they are in so battered a state that they are difficult to comprehend. Visitors should not attempt to inspect these because the structure is not entirely safe and for this reason the authorities have walled it off.

The level of the ground in front of the 'keep' has piled up over the centuries and

106

consequently one does not now have the impression of height which made this great pillared Propylaea loom above one. Originally this must have contributed greatly to its majestic effect.

The Temple itself was placed on an artificial hill, raised on the remains of an earlier one. When the whole Temenos was extended at the end of the second century A.D., the level of the central hill had to be continued out to the surrounding colonnades. This involved a massive filling operation which shows that the podium on which the Temenos walls stand was not only an architectural device to create a majestic appearance but a necessary retaining wall for the higher level within.

Inside the TEMENOS, one realises just how huge the precinct really is (Fig. 49). There is a tendency to forget that deep porticos ran completely round this wide, open space, creating a much greater impression of enclosure. Hardly a pillar stands of the northern portico, and it is much the same on the eastern side. Of the southern portico, however, there is a forest of golden sentinels with some long runs of entablature now back in place. Many of the pillars were re-erected by the Department of Antiquities in 1964. These three porticos, the north, east and south, were all built between A.D. 80 and 120 as evidenced by dedicatory inscriptions.

PALMYRA

Within the western portico was the inner wall of the Propylaea. The whole of this range was built in the middle of the second century A.D. and marks the final phase of construction in the Sanctuary. This was the age of the Antonines and the western range demonstrates the self-confidence and grandeur enjoyed in Palmyra at that time.

The colonnade on this side was interrupted by a central arch of great size which stood in front of the Propylaea. The pillars are higher than in the other three porticos, and the difference in scale can be clearly seen at the southern end where a stand of six marvellous Corinthian columns mark the junction of the porticos. The group is of great beauty with smooth, towering lines and sharpness of carving (Fig. 50). Their fullness and glowing colour make them one of the most rewarding sights

Fig. 49 Aerial view of the Sanctuary of Bel.

in the whole of Palmyra. The brackets which protrude from the shafts of each column, which the eminent archaeologist, Leonard Woolley, thought were 'a vulgar outrage on the constructional character of the column', occur on nearly all the pillars of Palmyra, and visitors will recognise them as one of the city's most distinctive features (Fig. 51).

Fig. 51 The colonnades on the south side of the Temenos.

g. **50** Pillars at the south-west corner of the Temenos.

Fig. 52 Reconstruction of the western colonnade of the Temenos showing the huge entrance portals in the Propylaea.

Fig. 53 The west side of the Temenos showing the inner façade of the Propylaea (now the Moslem Citadel).

The Propylaea wall with its three doorways would have been partly obscured from those standing in the Temenos. Once under the portico, this monumental composition would have been a striking and impressive counterpoint to the rhythm of pilasters which adorned the whole length of the wall on either side. All this is now lost, and a leap of imagination is required to visualise it as it was (Fig. 52). Even so the inner face of the Propylaea does still show the three entrances to the precinct, the centre one almost twice the size of those on either side (Fig. 53). One cannot but admire the boldness of the design, where a number of features of different scale are worked together with great skill to give a composition of richness, 'movement' and variety. It puts one in mind of Fourth Style wall paintings at Herculaneum, though this is not to suggest that the inspiration came from that quarter for, as Dr Lyttelton has pointed out, 'The Hellenistic traditions of Asia Minor and Alexandria appear to have been far more important than the

110

influence of Rome in forming the architectural style of Palmyra in the first century A.D.'* Combined with this is the luxuriant character of the Oriental tradition.

The western portico was one vast aisle, whereas all the other three were of two aisles, i.e. with an inner row of pillars. At the end of each inner colonnade there was a narrow spiral staircase which bored up within the thickness of a cluster of pilasters, giving access to the roof. The remains of such a stair are to be seen at the north-western corner.

* *Baroque Architecture in Classical Antiquity.*

Fig. 54 The north-west corner of the Temenos showing the holes in the masonry joints made during the Middle Ages when the metal clamps were mined out.

Fig. 55 The Ramp up which sacrificial animals were led into the Temenos.

Most visitors have commented on the countless holes in the joints in the masonry and pillars (Fig. 54). Metal clamps were used to lock the blocks together, but during the Islamic period these were mined out in an exhausting and exhaustive search for metal which seems to have halted at nothing. After all that effort one can only hope that a rusty old clamp was worth it.

Of particular interest in this north-western corner is the long RAMP, intersected on either side by wide flights of steps, which dives beneath a graceful and slender arch in the footings of the towering colonnade (Fig. 55). The springing of the arch is approximately on the vertical centre of the two columns above, which makes it look like a balancing act of great dexterity. Structurally it is perfectly sound, but it is yet another of those instances of seeming daring with which the Palmyrenes delighted themselves.

The ramp led under the pavement of the portico to a door in the outer wall of the Sanctuary through which the sacrificial animals were led (these would have been camels, bulls and rams but not swine).

Just beyond the point where the ramp reaches courtyard level are the remains of the SACRIFICIAL ALTAR. Only the basement and steps remain. They are confused with the foundations of a banqueting house and the possible line of the

112

original western wall of the Temenos. It would have been on this Altar platform that the Altar proper stood. Here the victims would have been offered and then burnt and their blood poured. Today most people regard blood sacrifice as a barbaric practice. The unpleasant side of the act, the pain and the suffering are stressed. Yet in ancient times sacrifice meant something very different. To the ancient world blood was the symbol of life, in fact was the source of life. By the use of blood in ritual sacrifice the congregation looked for renewal of life and, because blood was also the sole property of God, for renewal of divine protection and favour. By pouring of blood on the altar, blood was being rendered back to God. This mystical blood symbolism extends even into our time, for the Crucifixion, the supreme sacrifice, is perpetuated in the Communion service with the invitation to absolution and renewal of life in the words 'The Blood of our Lord Jesus Christ, which is shed for thee, preserve thy body and soul unto everlasting life'.

Immediately to the south of the Altar, placed symmetrically with it on the axis of the entrance to the temple, is the SACRED BASIN. Again only the lower courses remain, though here one can discern something of the plan. It was at this elevated, rectangular water tank that the officiating priests would ceremoniously and symbolically wash themselves and the sacred utensils. From here also would have been taken the 'consecrated' water for purification of the Altar. Even in the shadowy glimmers of half antiquity one finds the act of washing to be essential to the act of sacrifice. The risk of disease from unattended pools of blood would have been well known. It can be seen that a great many of the religious laws of antiquity were in essence health laws. From this ritual it was only a slight step for washing to take on a symbolic character even in public affairs, for example Pontius Pilate washing his hands.

The Abbé Starcky has pointed out a further confirmation of the Semitic plan of the whole Sanctuary, in that the arrangement of an altar for sacrifice and a sacred basin set before the temple proper recalls the Solomonic Temple in Jerusalem where there were the exactly similar Altar for Burnt Offerings and the Brazen Sea.

Standing in the centre of the Temenos is the TEMPLE OF BEL itself (Fig. 56). This was the first part of the Sanctuary to be built but it almost certainly stands on the site of an even earlier structure. Rostovtzeff felt certain that its curious plan and orientation were dictated by this earlier cella which he believed to have been Sumero-Babylonian. This cannot be substantiated until excavations below the temple are carried out. What are beyond question, however, are the date and dedication of the present building, for on the pedestal of a statue, now in the Museum, is the following inscription:

> In the month of October 357 (= A.D. 45) this is the statue of Lishamsh, son of Taibbol, son of Shokaibel of the Mene Komara: he has dedicated the Temple of the Gods Bel, Jarhibol and Aglibol in its sanctuaries, on the sixth day of April 343 (= A.D. 32); this statue has been erected by his sons to honour him.

Within the cella there are two large adytons, one in the north wall and one in the south. The sanctuaries mentioned in the inscription may well refer to these two adytons. The more important of the two was that in the north wall, which contained the effigies of the divine triad. In such circumstances one would have expected the entrance to be facing it, i.e. in the south wall, but this is occupied by the other adyton. The door was placed in the western wall, thus requiring a right angle in approach. This arrangement was most unusual in a Greek temple but the location of the principal shrine could have been dictated by its position in Rostovtzeff's Sumero-Babylonian temple. Had this been so it would have been unthinkable either to alter the orientation or to remove the shrine to a new location within the new building. It would have been impracticable to place the door in the south

Fig. 56 An aerial view of the Temple of Bel.

wall—even supposing that the south adyton could have been omitted—because this would have necessitated placing the Propylaea in the south colonnade which overlooks a steep and deep wadi.

It has been suggested that the door was sited off-centre in the west wall in order to provide greater room inside for rituals before the principal, northern, adyton. The result was to give a lop-sided effect to the façade outside.

The cella was raised on seven steps, a Greek krepis, above the level of the Temenos. However, when the Temenos was enlarged some of the necessary earth in-fill was obtained by lowering the level of the original courtyard. This had the effect of exposing the foundations of the krepis. To remedy this the krepis was

Fig. 57 Reconstruction of the Temple of Bel.

walled in, creating what is in fact a Roman podium without steps. Much of this podium has since disappeared and so today both arrangements are to be seen, often in juxtaposition.

The cella is only just over 13 metres wide, but originally the whole structure would have looked much fuller when surrounded by tall columns (Fig. 57). Only eight of these pillars are still standing, on the eastern side. The peristyle was very wide and spacious, with quite enough room to accommodate ritual processions round the temple. During the summer when the sun is almost directly overhead this deep peristyle would have provided much needed and pleasant shade. The peristyle was fifteen columns by eight columns, except for the west side where two bays were taken up by the huge entrance portal. The pillars are beautifully fluted, with blind fluting for the first metre (Plate 1). This blind fluting is well worth close inspection for the change in angle is so slight, and has to be so accurate if the illusion is to work, that one is delighted with the skill of the ancient masons. It is one thing to carve a deep capital, quite another to provide so subtle an effect as this where it seems that the thinnest muslin has been wrapped round the fluted column and the verticals still show through. This device probably came about of necessity.

116

Fig. 58 Garstang's photograph of the Sanctuary before clearance and excavation.

In crowded areas, such as the Stoa, the slender spines of the flutes could catch and bruise a passing arm far more easily than the smooth surface of a rounded column. So blind fluting was developed to protect those passing by without impairing the beauty of the pillars. It may even have been that the original answer was to wrap cloth or leather round the lower part until someone with a keen aesthetic eye saw the possibilities of a beautiful and practical architectural solution. Ritual processions round this peristyle would have had the idol carried in a palenquin of red leather, known as a Kobba. The attending flock of priests and acolites would doubtless have been grateful for the protection these blind flutes afforded.

Originally the columns were adorned with Corinthian capitals of gilded bronze, an effect of the greatest richness. Not an acanthus leaf or a scroll remains today; just the blank stone cores support the entablature. The architrave was boldly stepped; above this was a frieze of deeply carved winged and cloaked genii carrying garlands of fruit and fir cones. One or two blocks of this frieze are to be found arranged on the ground between the south-east corner of the temple and the east portico. The carving is not delicate, is in fact rather coarse, but it should be remembered that the frieze was intended to be seen high above one's head, in strong light, where fine detail and subtle nuances would be almost completely lost. Over this frieze projected a deep carved cornice.

Four of the crow-step merlons have been erected on top of the remaining section of the peristyle. The photograph by Garstang, taken in the 1920s, shows the peristyle without these merlons (Fig. 58).

117

The eastern, outside, wall of the cella was practically unadorned except for a wide, flat string course a metre and a half from the pavement, and for a series of framed and pedimented windows high up in the wall. Elegant pilasters emphasise the ends of the wall.

The south wall (Fig. 27) is a simple architectural composition of great clarity and purity. There is an almost classical restraint with two beautifully rendered Ionic half columns set between the two angle corner pilasters. Despite the buffeting of time and the metal-mining of men, this façade is well preserved. The Ionic capitals with their swirling volutes are beautifully done, as indeed is the carving on the corner pilasters. The balance between plain surface and carved detail—always a tricky thing—is just right, neither the detail nor the whole effect is overstated. The inspiration is wholly Greek, and the pleasing sense of repose is refreshing in a city where opulence was the keynote. This façade, like its counterpart on the north wall would have been enclosed in the peristyle, and so the effect we have today is rather different from that of ancient times.

The western wall contains the monumental entrance door. Set before this door is the colossal portal (Fig. 59) that was incorporated into the peristyle. Even though restored by Ecochard, it is still leaning out of plumb: nonetheless it is a remarkably dramatic piece of architecture. Approached by a very long flight of shallow, sloping steps—in effect a stepped ramp—it is richly carved with intertwining olives, vines and flowers. The whole portal takes up the space of two intercolumnations of the peristyle. Today it looks as if it were made up of a door frame with half columns on either side, but in its original context as an interruption of the rhythm of the colonnade (Fig. 57). It projects forward of the line of the peristyle and thus avoids the impression of being squashed between the columns. Above the carved, stepped architraves of the portal a cornice projected, supported on bold scrolled corbels at each side. Above the cornice additional half columns break forward over the vertical alignment of the door architraves which would have caused the principal cornice of the whole peristyle to break forward over the whole portal, thus emphasising once again the entrance. Dr Lyttelton has pointed out that 'The way in which it intrudes into the peristyle of the temple perhaps derives from a Ptolemaic scheme for articulation of temple façades, which is displayed in several small temples at Hermopolis in Lower Egypt; in these temples the doorway, together with its surrounds and projecting cornice, cuts into engaged columns decorating the façade of the temple.'* If this derivation is correct, then it is yet another piece of evidence of the strong cultural links with Egypt enjoyed by the Palmyrenes during the second half of the first century. What persuades the visitor today, however, is the masterly way in which the whole feature is handled as an

* *Baroque Architecture in Classical Antiquity.*

Fig. 59 The entrance portal to the Temple of Bel which was originally incorporated into the peristyle which surrounded the structure—see Fig. 57.

integral part of the whole façade. Without the sureness and self-confidence with which it is designed it could have been a dangerous introduction into the peristyle, ending up looking either inept or bombastic.

Huge stone beams linked the walls to the peristyle (Fig. 8) and on these the roofing blocks were laid. These beams were adorned with bas-reliefs which are of considerable interest. Two of them have been reconstructed on the ground close to the door of the temple. One shows the God Aglibol, a moon god, with the lunar crescent on his shoulders, wearing Roman costume, standing hand in hand over an altar with Malakbel, in this case a fertility deity. Associated schematically with Malakbel are pomegranates, pine cones and a kid; also a cypress tree was his emblem. To the left of the pair stand two Parthian worshippers.

Another relief depicts a camel carrying an enclosed tabernacle on its back attended by priests and worshippers. The group of completely veiled women (Fig. 6) who stand behind the camel is a marvellously expressive piece of art and one recognises these women as being caught up in a mystical experience. Quite apart from their expressive quality they are an interesting comment on the institution of veiled women long before Islam. The late Père de Vaux in his article on this subject showed that its origins lay in social demarcations which were later to be hallowed by the Moslem faith and thereby given religious significance (see pages 31 to 33).

From the architectural historical aspect, Seyrig drew attention to the oriental character of the iconographic reliefs in contrast to the classical styles of the vine decoration on the lower part of the beams. This is a good example of two artistic cultures working hand in hand, so often the case in Palmyra.

Another beam depicts the great Palmyrene triad of Gods standing in Roman dress (Fig. 8). Each panel of relief rested on a clearly carved egg and dart moulding, below which was a band with a footing of cyma reversa. Below this was a scroll of bunches of grapes with vine leaves and coils, on which even now some of the original colour remains. These were the 'bunches of vines' about which Dr Halifax was so enthusiastic. All these carvings were brightly coloured so that even in the shade of the peristyle they would have been quite distinguishable. The cyma reversa closely resembles the form of this decorative motif on Hellenistic buildings in Asia Minor: the temple of Artemis at Magnesia has a similar type, and the temple of Hecate at Lagina has an identical one as has the Round Temple in the Forum Boarium in Rome. Thus it appears that Hellenism, and not Rome, was the real cultural force during the first century A.D. in Palmyra.

On entering the Temple one is immediately aware of the cross-axis on which it is laid. The long walls of the cella are relatively plain, apart from two pairs of windows high up, with simple moulded frames, and a deep 'dado' rail a couple of metres from the pavement. It is possible that below this 'dado' the walls were clad in marble but this has now completely vanished.

The principal interest of the interior lies in the two adytons. The one to the north was the more important (Fig. 60) for it housed the images of the triad, Bel, Iarhibol and Aglibol. The Greeks and the Romans set their gods upon pedestals and the idea of putting the idols in a tabernacle or adyton is Syrian. The bi-cameral plan of the temple is Semitic with one adyton being the Holy of Holies and a second just Holy. This arrangement was to be found in the Temple of Jerusalem. Frequently

Fig. 60 The interior of the
Cella looking towards the
north, principal adyton.

Fig. 61 Architectural detail drawing of the
façade of the north adyton.

the two parts were divided off by a screen or curtain which was only drawn back at
given, short moments of a service. The division persists in present-day Orthodox
churches with the iconostasis. This attempt to surround the deity with an air of
mystery and apartness finds its roots in primitive sanctuaries.

It has been argued that the construction of the two adytons was undertaken after
the main fabric of the cella had been finished. The fact that the stonework is not
integrated into the main walls, nor is their design related at all closely to the rest of
the interior, tends to support this contention. Butler Murray held this view and
also pointed out the 'florid ornament of their ceilings'* as evidence of their belonging
to the second century A.D. or even to the time of Aurelian. However, analysis
of the sculptural detail establishes that they belong to the first century even though
they may not perhaps have been part of the original conception of A.D. 32.

The north adyton is a much more complex piece of architecture than it at first
appears. The façade is divided into three parts, the central one being a deep
tabernacle as a lodging for the effigies. The floor of this adyton is raised above that
of the cella and was possibly approached by a flight of steps. The architrave of the

* *Hellenistic Architecture in Syria*, Princeton, 1917.

opening cuts deeply into the flanking Ionic, fluted columns, indeed reduces them to quarter columns for much of their height. Only above the architrave do they appear as half columns backed by a quarter column (Fig. 61). We have seen this device before in the entrance portal in the peristyle where, because the feature is free-standing, the effect is much clearer. Here there is almost too much going on in a confined space. Above this, carried on pilasters, was a richly carved and ornamented entablature, stepped architrave, scroll frieze and elaborate cornice which extended from wall to wall. This ties the composition together, and the fact that the part over the central shrine is thrown forward helps to accentuate the overriding importance of the adyton below.

Flanking the central opening are niches with pilasters and pediments with acroteria. Above these pediments stand large representations of altars. The total height of this composition is lower than the architrave of the opening emphasising once again the importance of the adyton and always leading the eye to it.

The ceiling of the shrine (Fig. 62) is a monolith (single slab of stone) with a deeply carved cupola in which are the signs of the seven planets, with Jupiter in the centre. Round these are ranged the twelve signs of the Zodiac. The soffit of the lintel is adorned with the spread eagle of Jupiter in a star-filled sky. This indicates Jupiter/Bel presiding over the celestial movements and, through their agency, over the fortunes of men. Behind the wall to the left a stairway leads up to the roof, from which there is a fine view out over the Temenos and beyond.

The façade of the south adyton is clearer and less complicated, yet perhaps for that it is not quite so interesting or successful. It consists of an engaged four pillar portico with the entablature projecting forward. The central bay is considerably wider than those flanking it, even so the huge opening to the shrine still eats into the two central pillars, reducing them in their lower part to mere quarter columns. The cornice on top of the entablature cuts right across these quarter columns which therefore become detached from their upper parts: even more disturbing is the way the upper parts are not vertically aligned with those below. The two outer half columns rise to their full height without interruption and seem rather lost. However, it has been suggested that the portico was originally capped by a pediment which would certainly have resolved the composition and would in particular have given the flanking half columns some point. Approached by a broad stepped ramp similar to the one outside, the whole central feature must have been very impressive. It is the absence of the main cornice and the conjectured pediment that tends to throw the composition and make the door architrave seem overbearing and squat (Fig. 63).

This adyton probably housed the portable image of Bel which could be carried around the Sanctuary on feast days. It has been suggested by the Abbé Starcky that, when in the adyton, the idol may have been laid on a bed of the type so

Fig. 62 The drawing by Wood and Dawkins of the ceiling of the north adyton—the so-called 'Zodiac ceiling'.

Fig. 63 Architectural detail drawing of the façade of the south adyton.

123

frequently found in Palmyrene sculpture. This is clearly shown on a tessera (an invitation tablet to a religious ritual banquet in honour of the deity).

The glory of the south adyton is the monolith ceiling (Figs. 64 and 38) which, although now much blackened by smoke, is remarkably well preserved with its detail still as crisp as when first done. This was the ceiling which so excited Wood and Dawkins and the design of which had such an effect on English architecture during the second half of the eighteenth century. A large fleuron of acanthus and

Fig. 64 The monolith south adyton ceiling which, though much blackened, has remarkably well preserved carved detail.

Fig. 65 Garstang's photograph of the entrance portal to the Temple before the Temenos was cleared of the mud-brick houses which had engulfed it.

lotus leaves dominates the middle of the design, round which there is a broad band of meander. This is then set in a square with deeply cut spandrels. Round this there is a series of octagonal coffers, containing rosettes, held together by a complicated geometry of squares and triangles. These 'fuse into an unending series of elaborate geometric patterns'.* It is a marvellously co-ordinated design and a staggering exercise in mathematics. The sensitivity and fineness of the detail are marshalled with much skill.

The Islamic period has left its mark on the interior of the cella with some important and interesting inscriptions. The cella was turned into a mosque and only ceased serving as such with the grand clearance of the whole Sanctuary in 1929 (Fig. 65). On the rear wall of the north adyton there is one of the earliest Islamic inscriptions dating from 110 A.H. (A.D. 728–29). It is in Archaic Cufic and reads: 'May God take pity on Abd as-Samad, son of Obeid, and on Muhammed, son of Yazid, and forgive them their sins, old and recent; written in the year 110.

* *Baroque Architecture in Classical Antiquity.*

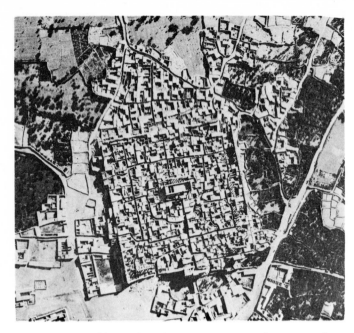

Fig. 66 Aerial view showing the Arab village within the Sanctuary walls.

Fig. 67 The remains of an Exedra on the Colonnade Street between the Sanctuary of Bel and the Monumental Arch.

May God take pity on anyone who says after reading this: Amen.' This inscription was published by M. Sauvaget in conjunction with the Amir Djafar al-Hassani in his *Inscriptions of Palmyra*.

As has been related, the cella was turned into a mosque in the twelfth century and this accounts for a Mihrab inscription in the south adyton, which states that it was carried out by al-Nasseh Yussuf ibn Mousa on the orders of the Sultan al-Malik al-Mujahed (635 A.H.).

Finally, opposite the main door is a long edict dated 868 A.H. (A.D.1463), by the governor of Damascus, Al Zahir Baibars, reaffirming the rights of the inhabitants of Palmyra to graze their cattle on Mount Terebinth to the south-west of the oasis, and to do so without interference. There are other devotional graffiti scratched on the walls.

It is not long ago that the whole Sanctuary was thickly packed with mud-brick houses set around winding alleys. There is an interesting aerial photograph (Fig. 66) of it in this state with an overspill clustering outside the walls. The walls and central cella are clearly distinguishable amid the tangle of streets and box-like houses. It was only in 1929 when the new town of Palmyra/Tadmor was built that the villagers were able to move and it became possible for the French archaeologist, Amy, to clear the whole sanctuary. There are some photographs by Garstang now in the archives of the Palestine Exploration Fund which show the ruins still ensnared with the mud-brick houses (Figs. 19, 58 and 65). Some of them remind one of William Par's drawings of Athens and Asia Minor during the Ottoman period, with battered columns erupting strangely out of a backyard, colonnades suffocating in a sea of mud-brick, romantic and indescribably horrid.

126

Save when a charabanc disgorges its camera-clicking, gum-chewing passengers, who are yelled at incoherently by a fraught guide, the Sanctuary of Bel is a place of peace and quiet. It is a golden place in which to wander and explore. Long wire grass, thistles and wild thyme compete with fragments of the past for a basking place in the sun. Cog-wheel slices of fluted columns lie arranged or in disorder, forming fantastic vistas of twisting perspective (Plate 3).

Outside the Sanctuary stands the derelict building of the old Palmyra Museum, and a little to the north the ruinous remains of a rather palatial Arab residence.

From in front of the Propylaea there stretched in antiquity a very wide colonnaded avenue to the Monumental Arch which can be seen a short way off. The width of the avenue was the same as the full width of the arch which was designed to serve as the climax. The area in front of the Propylaea has never been excavated but Rostovtzeff considered that the broad avenue could be likened to a dromos of a Babylonian temple. As it is, the road to the new town cuts across the line of the old colonnaded avenue and there is nothing to see until one comes to four tall pillars standing in grand isolation (Fig. 67).

This is all that remains of an imposing EXEDRA, the pillars of which have been re-erected by the Department of Antiquities. They formed a portico projecting forward of, and considerably higher than, those on the line of the main colonnade. The central opening is wider than the flanking pair and the deep curve of the wall behind was decorated with niches framed by slender columns and a 'Syrian' pediment. These 'Syrian' pediments are a very common feature in Palmyra, occurring in the Theatre, Diocletian's Camp, the Monumental Arch and elsewhere. They are always richly carved and have, despite their elaborateness, a light airiness which reminds one yet again of Pompeian wall paintings. The four pilasters behind are not properly aligned with the four main columns. This raises the problem of how the exedra was roofed—if at all. Was it that the four pillars were completely free-standing, with statues on their tops, rather like votive columns? Or did they carry an entablature that was returned right back to the rear wall.

The massive paving slabs are still in place and were uncovered when the authorities cleared the site and re-erected the pillars. At the same time the row of bases stretching towards the Arch was revealed and established the character of this vanished section of the Colonnade Street (Fig. 68). Behind this colonnade were shops and other premises, some of which have also been cleared out.

The fourth opening along towards the Arch is a doorway of larger size and more important character than the others. It obviously led to a building of consequence, but this is at present unexcavated. So often in these ancient sites one comes across a fine doorway through which one is faced with a wall of earth. Archaeologists take time—it is an essential part of their discipline—and spectators will just have to be patient however tantalising the imagination makes such doorways.

Fig. 68 Pavement detail of the Exedra,
showing the line of the street colonnade
beyond, indicated by the straight
run of bases of pillars.

Beyond this there is a simple entrance with two free-standing pillars which gives
into a small Nymphaeum, at the back of which is a water tank.

A narrow street curves off to the left just past this, giving access to various
dwellings and possibly a small baths complex. The pattern of walls, doors, rooms
and tiny courtyards is intriguing though the arrangement is very confused.

Fig. 69 The Monumental Arch drawn by Wood and Dawkins.

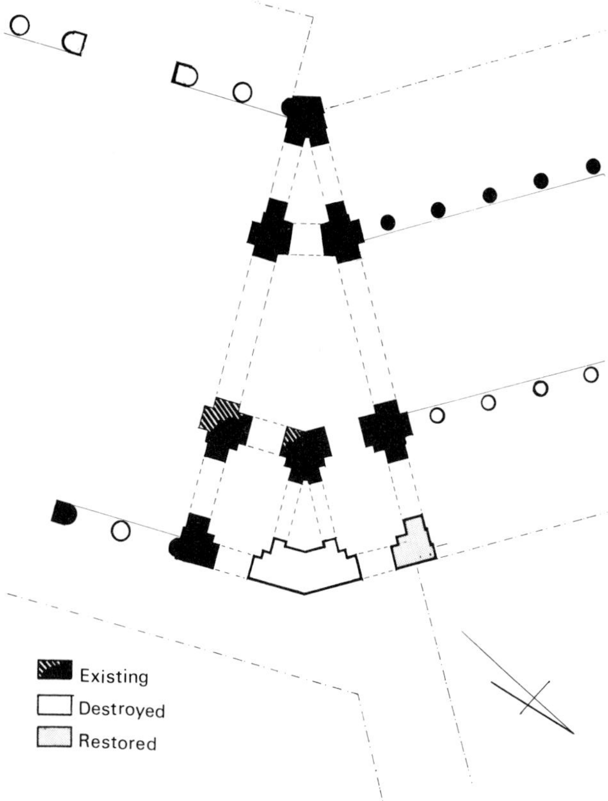

Fig. 71 The joint springing of the side arches at the pivot of the plan.

Existing
Destroyed
Restored

Fig. 70 Plan of the Monumental Arch.

PALMYRA TODAY

ZONE TWO

*The Monumental Arch, Temple of Nebo, Central Colonnade Street, Baths of Diocletian,
First Transverse Street, Gate with Niches and South Wall, and The Theatre*

The MONUMENTAL ARCH is probably the most famous monument of Palmyra
and is certainly the most frequently illustrated. From Wood and Dawkins, who
made considerable play of it (Fig. 69), to the picture postcards of today, it is its
pictorial aspect that is all-important. This is not surprising for it was a conscious
piece of pictorial design. As described in the previous chapter it masks a thirty
degrees bend at the point in the Colonnade Street where it turns southwards on the
final, wide last leg towards the Sanctuary of Bel. Its plan is 'V' shaped (Fig. 70) so
that each façade is placed at right angles to its respective street. The form is a large,
high central arch flanked by a lower arch on either side, an arrangement very
reminiscent of the Triumphal Arch of the Roman Imperial Period. The flanking
arches on the north-west façade were located under the porticos which lined each
side of the street, whereas those on the south-west façade formed an integral part of
the triple arch concept, with the colonnades set at the extreme points of the whole
structure. The way in which the transition between the two arrangements is
handled is one of the marvels of the structure.

The two façades start from the same point, the point of the 'V'. At the central
arch, the distance between these façades is wide enough to admit a transverse arch
(Fig. 71) which thus becomes part of the south-western wall of the big central arch.

Fig. 72 The junction of the main
leg of the Colonnade Street
and the Monumental Arch: note
the richness of the carving.

Fig. 73 Garstang's photograph of the soffit of one of the side arches showing the variety of carved detail.

It is suitably decorated with a pedimented niche above it. The opposite wall of the central arch shows the change in direction of the street with a shallow angle. In place of the single arch in the south-west wall there are two arches of comparable size which are also surmounted by pedimented niches. Behind these lie the north-eastern side arches providing access to an unexcavated street.

It is a cunning architectural arrangement which had considerable theatrical effect (Fig. 33). Dr Lyttelton rightly likens it to a stage set by Bibbiena, for it is essentially a piece of 'decor' even though it is integrated into the design of the two streets which approach it. On the south-eastern side the pilasters which received the last section of the entablature of the colonnade are a part of the design, being of the same height and scale as the pilasters which carry the big central arch. The junction on the north-western side is particularly noteworthy for the imagination at work behind it (Fig. 72). Against the wall of the Arch there is an elaborate Corinthian capital resting on a palmetted console supported by a lion's mask. Below this the pilaster is panelled with an intertwining floral and leaf design. This decorative, floral panelling is of amazing variety; hardly two panels have exactly the same treatment. It is the extraordinary wealth of carved detail allied to the virtuosity of the purely architectural concept which is more than half the glory of this Arch. This richness of detail extends from the hoods of the arches—which are particularly beautiful—to the soffits of the arches where instead of ordinary rosetted coffers one has a bewildering array of geometric patterns (Fig. 73). The niches have base plinths whose projecting ends supported miniature columns over which are entablatures whose cornices correspondingly project. The open pediment concludes the theme (Fig. 74).

Fig. 74 The 'Syrian niches' within the central opening of the Monumental Arch.

Fig. 75 The ruins of the Temple o Nebo.

However, at no stage does the carved detail take over from the architecture; it is strictly controlled and concentrated in clearly defined and appropriate places. The architectural feeling of this Arch is very strong and the carved detail tends to emphasise this. Perhaps it is the appropriateness of all the detail and the fact that there is much open space within the structure, which makes it so three-dimensional. This Arch is very much an exercise in enclosed space rather than in solid form.

Schlumberger has suggested that the Arch and the central section of the Colonnade Street date from the late second century. This he bases on an analysis of the style of the Corinthian capitals: most of the inscriptions on the brackets of the pillars date from the third century but this is regarded only as an upper limit for the dating. The whole structure was extensively restored and stabilised by Amy in 1931.

To the left of the Arch lie the ruins of the TEMPLE OF NEBO (Fig. 75). This was uncovered by the Department of Antiquities in 1963, although Wiegand had put down some exploratory trenches upon which he based his plan of the site. The three successive seasons of work by the Department have provided a corrected

134

plan. Considering the scope of Wiegand's work and the absence of archaeological evidence it is remarkable that he was so accurate. His plan was accompanied by drawn and written notes which state the limit of the evidence upon which he was working.

Nebo was the son of Mardok, Lord of Heaven in the Babylonian pantheon. There he was considered the secretary of the gods and as such held considerable sway over human destinies. But in Palmyra his classical counterpart was Apollo even though he was always linked with Bel, their names appearing jointly on tesserae. His Babylonian origins show an interesting link with the eastern world—a link which permeated every aspect of Palmyrene life, its architecture, religion, sculpture and social order.

PALMYRA

The plan of the Sanctuary (Fig. 76) is another case of a peristyled cella set within a porticoed Temenos. We have already seen this arrangement—but on a vastly different scale—in the Sanctuary of Bel. The entrance or Propylaea to the Temenos on the west side was adorned with a portico of six plain columns *in antis* approached by three steps. Behind this was the main door which was decorated with beautifully fluted engaged half columns (Fig. 77). Through this one was confronted by a large and elaborate altar with a group of three miniature columns at each corner.

Behind the altar stood the temple, standing on its podium (Fig. 78). A flight of wide steps led up from the Temenos through a break in the podium. The peristyle was Corinthian—Wiegand termed this 'The Corinthian Temple'—and encircled the whole cella. None of this is now standing; in fact the ruins are rather sparse and low with no verticals left.

The Temenos was colonnaded on three sides only, the rear side, that which backs onto the Colonnade Street, having had its portico cut off when the street was laid out in its present form (see page 84). Inscriptions found during excavations indicate that the Temple was built at approximately the same time as the cella of the Temple of Bel. On the southern side, near the Propylaea, there are various rooms which could possibly have been for the use of the college of priests who administered the rites at the shrine.

South of the Temenos there is a structure which has not yet been cleared. All that remains is the podium and the first courses of its walls showing the bases of the pilasters which adorned the façade. The so-called 'Zenobia' wall was built into the side of this structure making it a bastion; this happened to several monuments along the line of the wall. It was evidently a building of some pretensions to merit the architectural treatment it was given, which is not dissimilar to that of the Baal Shamin Sanctuary. It could be a house or temple tomb but until it has been excavated it must remain one of the many unanswered questions of Palmyra.

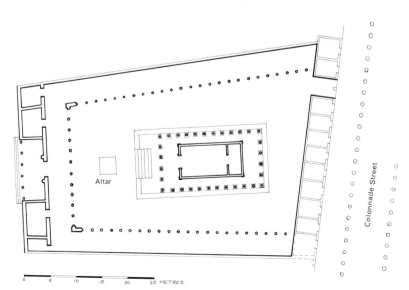

Altar

Colonnade Street

Fig. 76 The plan of the Sanctuary of Nebo.

0   5   10   15   20   25 METRES

Fig. 77 Reconstruction of the Propylaea to the Sanctuary of Nebo.

Fig. 78 Reconstruction of the Temple of Nebo.

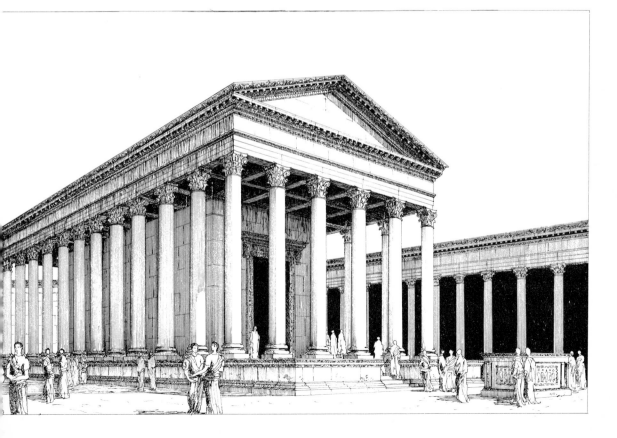

The central arm of the COLONNADE STREET (Figs. 79 and 80) is its best preserved section with a regiment of pillars lined up for inspection. Beneath the porticos were shops, many of which still carry the name and trade of the proprietor on the lintel over the door. Half-way up each column there are the familiar brackets for statues projecting over the roadway which would have added an extra effect of richness to an already grandiose conception. Those brackets nearest the Arch never received their statues; presumably their installation was cut short by Aurelian's suppression of the Zenobia revolt in A.D. 272. There was time enough, however, for eight statues of Worog, Governor of the city at the time of Odainat and Zenobia, to be put in place. Schlumberger dates this part of the Colonnade Street to the late second century as part of the civic aggrandisement which accompanied the period of the city's greatest prosperity and expansion (Fig. 32).

There is still an atmosphere of splendour, with golden columns bearing the scars of history and the sores of time. A timeless silence steals through the colonnades teasing the imagination with half-stated facts, but these colonnades are tight-lipped like the bereaved, full of the secrets of the past. They have felt the heat of countless summer suns, stood before the sandy blasts of spring winds and the frosts of winter so that they now radiate an immutable experience of centuries.

g. 79 The drawing by Wood
d Dawkins of the Colonnade
reet as it was circa 1751 which,
comparison with Fig. 80,
ows how much has survived.

Fig. 80 The main leg of the
Colonnade Street looking towards
the Monumental Arch.

Across the street, on the north side, stand four tall, monolithic porphyry columns on pedestals. The two outer ones are backed by square pillars to which are attached half columns marking the place where the main colonnade joined this impressive portico (Fig. 81). Behind these square pillars are the springings of arches which once spanned the interior of the portico. The whole is raised a step above the pavement level, giving it a little more emphasis. This structure, which has been partly reassembled, is the entrance to the BATHS OF DIOCLETIAN erected during that emperor's reign (A.D. 284–305) by the then Governor of Syria, Sosianus Hierocles. The warm pink-grey of the columns is one of the very few intrusions of coloured stone in a city which was otherwise built of the local pale gold limestone. It is this consistency of colour which gives apparent homogeneity to the ruins of Palmyra.

Above the porphyry columns was an entablature probably crowned with a pediment of which nothing remains today.

The site was excavated by the Syrians in 1959–60, revealing a large central pool, several other smaller bath chambers, a large octagonal 'meeting room', stove area and more importantly a covered aqueduct. The so-called 'meeting room' still has its huge paving slabs in place with a drain in the centre of the room. Hardly

Fig. 81 The portico of the Baths of Diocletian.

Fig. 82 The sunken bath in the Diocletian complex.

anything of the walls now stands, and so there is no sense of the original feeling of enclosure. To judge from the obvious use of water in this room, it is more likely to have been a bath chamber or changing room (*apodyterion*) than a meeting room. Certainly Baths in Roman times were frequently furnished with libraries, gymnasia and exercise rooms as well as chambers for lectures and discourses. The position of this octagonal room to the right of the main entrance axis and its evident importance leads one to suspect that it was not an actual bath chamber but served one of these subsidiary purposes.

Beyond is the principal pool, possibly the Frigidarium or cold bath, surrounded by a colonnade of Corinthian columns. This peristyle has stood the test of time for it appears in all pictures of the site from Hofstede to modern photographs. The pillars have been patched where blown sand has dangerously eroded their lower shafts but they are otherwise as they have always been.

Steps lead down into the pool (Fig. 82) and it is probable that the sides were clad in marble. Needless to say, nothing of this now remains. The general plan of the complex does not conform to the standard Roman type as epitomised by the Baths of Caracalla in Rome or, if one must have a provincial example, by the superb

Hadrianic Baths at Leptis Magna. At this late date it was probably necessary to accommodate it into an existing plot of land, disposing the rooms without any adherence to a formal plan. However, the aqueduct would have caused considerable upheaval if it had to be laid under adjacent properties. It could be, therefore, that the present structure replaced a previous Baths on the site.

To the west of the central pool are the incomplete excavations of what were the boiler or furnace rooms for there is much evidence of burning as well as fragments of a brick hypocaust.

Nearby, opposite the portico of the Diocletian Baths, there is a wide arch marking the point at which a transverse street joined the main thoroughfare (see page 84). The colonnade was stopped with an engaged half column against a full height pilaster, on the other side of which was the impost and springing of the arch (Fig. 83). These arches are wide, so their springing had to be relatively low. The keystone lies immediately below the architrave of the colonnade which extended continuously over it. Note the beautiful attention to detail on the arch, particularly the characteristic 'palm tree' frieze which sweeps up to a delightful little flower rosette. Behind the arch, in the rear wall of the portico was a corresponding arch of identical character which gave into the side street (Fig. 31). In this case the TRANSVERSE STREET was also colonnaded—at least on one side. The original effect must have been very dramatic and attractive; from the bright sunlight of the street looking through the shade of double arches to another line of sunlit pillars set at right angles to the main thoroughfare. Here the effect would have been greatly enhanced by the eventual curve of the transverse street as it swept round the back of the auditorium of the Theatre.

This area has been substantially cleared, and one can still gain a good impression of what it must have been like. Behind the curve, the colonnade turns abruptly to the south across uncleared ground. The first few pillars are fallen and their remains buried, but further on ten still stand proudly bearing their full entablature, their brackets within touching distance of the ground.

This colonnade ends in an imposing GATE. This has been partly cleared of sand, revealing the well preserved lower part, whereas the top part which has always been exposed has suffered badly with all detail virtually obliterated (Fig. 84). The single, central opening was spanned by an arch, on either side of which were two engaged half columns with a niche set high between them. Panels of leaf and flower ornament decorate the two outer imposts of each section. The South Wall which was built against each side of the arch structure is not integrated into its stonework. There is no architectural continuation of detail for the moulding of the base returns into the thickness of the wall at the extremities. This leads one to suspect that this archway was perhaps more of a Triumphal Arch, marking the approach to the formally planned city centre. When the present South Wall was

Fig. 83 The intersection of a side street with t
main Colonnade Street—compare with Fig. 3

Fig. 84 The so-called 'Caravan Gate' at the end of
the Transverse Street behind the Theatre.

built the arch was used as a ready-made porte and the wall was thus aligned on it.
It should not be forgotten that the ancient city extended considerably further to the
south than the present limits described by this South, the so-called 'Zenobia',
Wall (see Map 3). The Gate probably dates from shortly after the completion
of the central Colonnade Street, i.e. the middle of the second century A.D.

The SOUTH WALL extends all along the southern side of the city centre, often
cutting into buildings or using them as adjuncts to itself. It extends from the
Damascus Gate near Diocletian's Camp to just beyond the Temple of Nebo. As
explained in the previous chapter, it was put together with material from dismantled buildings. It is not known whether this was part of Zenobia's fortifications
after the collapse of her revolt against Rome. It certainly has the appearance of
being hastily constructed on a position overlooking a shallow wadi which would

Fig. 85 The *cavea* of the Theatre—originally there were as many as thirty rows of seats.

have made it a formidable obstacle. By its construction a major section of the city was cut off, leaving the northern half within the safety of the walls.

It is worth descending into the wadi at this point and ascending the opposite bank, for one sees very clearly the full extent of the wall and how it made use of the stately buildings it met in its course. Possibly the most dramatic distortion is to be found in the handsome portico of the Tariff Court which is rendered utterly pointless by the wall in front of it.

Returning to the city centre one comes to the rear of the Theatre. To inspect this large monument it is best to go back via the curved Colonnade Street to the double arches by the main thoroughfare.

Opinions vary as to the date of the THEATRE. Schlumberger suggests the late second century A.D. whilst Michalowski places it earlier, in the first half of that century. It is of the standard Roman, as opposed to Greek, model with a semi-circular *orchestra* 20 metres in diameter, above which rises the *cavea* of the auditorium. At present there are nine rows of seats divided into eleven *cunei* or sections (Fig. 85). In its original form this *cavea* was considerably higher; Wiegand's reconstruction shows thirty rows of seats in three storeys rising to a pillared loggia on the highest level. This extended *cavea* would have come fairly close to the curved Colonnade Street. However, none of this was found when the

Fig. 86 The stage of the Theatre.

Theatre was uncovered in 1952, and any reconstruction must perforce be conjectural. Separating the rising levels of the *cavea* from the flagged floor of the *orchestra* is a strong screen-wall which describes the complete half circle. The flagstones are set diagonally and are retained by a single step platform in front of the screen-wall. On this platform would have been placed the seats for distinguished spectators, members of the Senate and other leaders, both religious and temporal. The end blocks to the screen-wall are roughly in the shape of a side of a chair.

Facing the *cavea* is the stage (Fig. 86) above which rise the remains of the *scaenae frons* or stage wall. The front of the stage might originally have been clad in marble and been adorned with eleven panels of sculpture; these panels being rectangular

146

Fig. 87 Reconstruction of the stage and
scaenae frons of the Theatre.

and curved alternately. There are many instances of this in the late Hellenistic/
Roman world, possibly the finest existing series being in Sabratha in Libya.

The *scaenae frons* has the standard three doors onto the stage from behind with
the addition of two smaller ones on either flank. The central door, the *porta regia*, is
the largest and is set in an exedra, whereas this is normally semi-circular, here it is
a half-oval. The half-oval is lined with six free-standing columns. The recesses for
the other two doors are rectangular, and the columns of the half-oval turn into
these recesses only to break forward again into the main cross axis where they
extend to the limits of the *scaenae frons*. There is a continuous entablature providing
a strong unifying effect horizontally across the whole composition. Over the doors
were niches, equipped with miniature pillars and pediments, and with shell heads.
The two small doors on the extreme ends were surmounted by two niches, one
upon the other. Flanking the *porta regia* were four columns, much larger than the
others, two on either side, one behind the other. This would have given particular
emphasis to the central feature (Fig. 87). It is probable that the whole arrangement, with the exception of the four columns in the centre, was repeated on a
second floor, giving the effect of a forest of pillars undulating across the curved and

147

rectangular wall on two levels. Architectural detail was, as always, sumptuously carved.

This is a strikingly 'baroque' design and the sense of 'movement' has great momentum. The constant breaking forward of the entablature, the change from rectangular to the curve, and the strong vertical and horizontal emphases all amount to a piece of great visual excitement. The effect today is rather lost due to its dilapidated state, but one can still sense the contrasts. The effect of one scale set within another is the main counterpoint of the *scaenae frons*. The bold, solid podium on which the composition stands marks out the principal theme, but above rises a virtuoso series of harmonious variations.

Behind the *scaenae frons* the doors gave directly into the south portico of the Colonnade Street. Consequently the 'green rooms' must have been to the sides of the stage; there is in fact a series of rooms on the western side which could have served these purposes. It would seem possible therefore, that when there was a performance in progress the portico was used as part of the theatre with screens set up temporarily in this area. The rear wall was, however, treated architecturally with pilasters aligned with the pillars of the Colonnade Street (Fig. 88).

If Michalowski is correct in dating the Theatre to the first half of the second century then it is earlier than the Colonnade Street which it abuts. The implications of this are significant, for if this is so, the Theatre would have dictated the angle for the change in direction of the Colonnade Street. This would account for the absence of rooms behind the stage. Certainly the town planners were not above lopping off the northern portico of the peristyle round the Sanctuary of Nebo but to have destroyed the stage and *scaenae frons* of the Theatre would have meant a complete remodelling of the whole structure—perhaps an expense which not even Palmyra would entertain.

Fig. 88 Behind the *scaenae frons*, the area inside the once covered portico on the west side of the Colonnade Street.

Fig. 89 Booths on the side street which leads from the Colonnade Street to the Senate and the Tariff Court.

ZONE THREE

The Senate, the Agora, the Nymphaeum, the Tariff Court, the Corinthian Peristyle, the Zenobia Inscription, the Tetrapylon and the Second Transverse Street

Facing the west side of the Theatre is a row of small booths, the interiors of which have not yet been fully excavated. Their imposts and lintels are mostly intact and they form an attractive small scale façade (Fig. 89). To the right of these booths is another double arch bringing one back into the Colonnade Street. Across the foot of the forward arch is a broken section of the clay and stone aqueduct (Fig. 90) which can be traced for a considerable way towards the Monumental Arch. It is constructed of many stone units, through which ran the water pipe. The blocks are lifted off the ground a foot or so and are quite obviously a later intrusion. This aqueduct dates from the period after the decline of the city when one must assume the original water system had failed. With the decline one can understand that there were not the funds available to make a neat job of the aqueduct by sinking it

149

below the pavement. Perhaps also there was a feeling of hopelessness amongst the civic authorities who were hard pressed to maintain even a semblance of amenities without having to worry about the niceties of a concealed water system. The aqueduct was probably laid down during the reign of the Byzantine Emperor Justinian (A.D. 527–65). The eastern trade had lost its momentum, and control by the Imperial authorities rapidly weakened. The opulent and fabled city of Palmyra became an obvious target for plunderers and therefore Justinian also strengthened the so-called 'Zenobia' wall, though one wonders quite what military advantage there was in transforming every fourth tower in the east wall into a semi-circular one: a laborious operation.

Looking back from the double arch and aqueduct one sees a row of eight pillars, all truncated, with a high wall behind (Fig. 90). This is an area of great interest and importance in the study of Palmyra.

The pillars were the portico of the SENATE which lies immediately behind. It is a small building with a central peristyle approached through an 'entrance hall', with an apsidal chamber on the opposite side. Another, square, room was to the left. The site is roughly triangular with the eastern wall following the same curve as the back of the auditorium of the Theatre. It was Seyrig who identified it as the Senate, the debating house of the governing body of the city, and parallels can be found for it in other parts of Asia Minor, notably at Dura-Europos, with whose fortunes Palmyra was intimately connected.

Before the accession of Hadrian in A.D. 117, the decisions and power of the Senate were probably strongly influenced by a military governor appointed from Rome. Even so two *archons* fulfilled the post which was equivalent to that of a present-day mayor. These were later to assume the title of *strategi* and would have been responsible with the other Senators for much of the domestic running of the city's affairs. It must be remembered that Palmyra was not just a city but a city-state which served as a buffer between Rome and Parthia, maintaining the precarious balance of peace and communication between the two fronts. Rome usually respected the limited independence of the city-state so as to maintain its neutrality. The measure of Roman control in the affairs of the city would have reflected the state and atmosphere of Imperial politics. With growing unrest within the Empire during the third century, effective control of these affairs weakened and laid the situation open to those who sought personal power. The danger was already apparent even in the time of Hadrian for, in an attempt to control through privilege, Rome acquiesced in the rule of the Senate by a Ras or leader. This control worked only so long as Rome remained the fount of privilege. When an underlying contempt for Roman honours set in, the path was open for overt personal ambition. Thus was Odainat able to assume the title of King. He was wise enough, perhaps honourable enough as well, to contain his ambition. He

Fig. 90 Looking down the side street from the Colonnade Street towards the Senate and Tariff Forum. On the ground a section of the water duct believed to have been installed during the Byzantine period.

could have aspired to Valerian's Imperial crown, but probably sensing that, quite rightly, the turmoil at the time was still fluid enough to permit Roman influence to reassert itself, he actively supported the Emperor. His reward was to come from Valerian's son, the Emperor Gallienus, who bestowed on him the title 'Corrector of all the East'. This invested him, as the Abbé Starcky has put it, 'with extraordinary civil and especially military powers'. Odainat's ambition broadened when, after the defeat of the Sassanians, he adopted the title 'King of Kings', the traditional title of the ancient kings of Babylon. His wife, the fabled Zenobia, was less circumspect with the known result.

When looking at the scanty remains of what appears to have been a diminutive structure by Palmyrene standards, it is well to remember the intrigue and political in-fighting which this small chamber must have witnessed. Within its walls were the high decisions of state forged; what tales could these worn flagstones tell.

Fig. 91 The Tariff Court from in front of the Senate.

Outside the Senate, to its south, is a huge walled enclosure (Fig. 91). It is not yet known exactly what purpose this monumental space served but in it was found the Palmyrene Tariff (see page 15) and in consequence it is known as the TARIFF COURT or TARIFF FORUM. The main entrance was on the southern side where three large doorways lead into a monumental portico *in antis*: two of the doorways still have their lintels. The portico is sadly dilapidated and its plan much confused by the 'Zenobia' wall which runs across the front of it. This portico must originally have faced out onto a worthy approach but at present no excavations have been made into the sand dunes, so we have no way of telling its character.

Clearly this was a monumental entry into a structure of great importance. The whole treatment is majestic (Fig. 92). The south wall, the entry wall, has bold pilasters carrying a full entablature, all now much eroded, whilst the crowning cornice is completely missing. Between the doorways are the remains of wide brackets which possibly carried pillared niches in the Palmyrene manner, though there are no indications on the stonework of any pediment or responding pilasters. It could, however, have been that in these brackets there were originally statuary groups.

Fig. 92 The Tariff Court. Originally
this important area was approached
through a monumental portico on the
other side of the end wall: much of
this was destroyed with the construction
of the so-called 'Zenobia wall'.

Fig. 93 The Tariff Court by L.–F.
Cassas showing the left hand wall still
standing.

The flanking walls, to the east and west, were likewise adorned with pilasters between which, certainly on the western side, were windows with strongly moulded architraves carrying richly ornamented pediments. The eastern wall is no longer standing but the drawing by L.-F. Cassas (Fig. 93) done in the 1790s shows that it was identical. The windows of the western wall look through into the impressive Agora. The architraves and pediments on the Tariff Court side are severely weathered but enough is there for one to capture the original richness of effect.

The northern wall which backed onto the Senate has fallen forward on its face and lies with each block correctly in place beside its neighbour. It would not be too exacting a task to re-erect this wall, which would go a long way to recreating the sense of enclosure. The cost of such an exercise might be considerable, but the Syrian authorities have a fine record of reinstatement amongst the ruins, so it is to be hoped that their attention might one day turn to this fallen wall. The point of entry at the north-western corner presents a tantalising problem, for if there had been a door of any consequence—as one would expect—then there should be evidence of it on the stonework of the western wall. There is none. How then was this corner closed, if at all? It lies very close to the southern end of the Senate portico and would have played an important part in the, as yet unexcavated, scheme for the area north of the Agora. There is also the question of levels, for the small north-eastern door into the Agora is lower than the Senate portico. Until this area has been cleared and excavated there can be no answer to the problem.

To the west of the Tariff Court lies the AGORA (Figs. 94 and 16), with what is called the Senators' Gate connecting the two. Seyrig and Duru began excavations here in 1939, and what has been revealed establishes the Agora as one of the most significant public structures in Palmyra. This vast rectangle (48 × 71 metres) is surrounded by a Corinthian portico on all four sides; many of the pillars are still standing, though sadly most are truncated. Strangely enough it was in a fairly ruinous state even in the time of Zenobia, for materials from here were employed in building the wall attributed to her. Quite enough remains both of the pillars and the enclosing wall for us to appreciate the scale and effect of this monument. Garstang's photograph (Fig. 95) showing the Agora in its unexcavated state is most interesting for, when compared with recent photographs, it shows something of the huge task facing archaeologists in such circumstances.

The Agora was the public meeting place and is a feature common to all Graeco-Roman cities. One can imagine the comings and goings and the buzz of conversation with groups of people earnestly or casually exchanging news.

From each pillar projected the ubiquitous bracket upon which stood a statue of some worthy: the attendant inscriptions have been deciphered, giving us valuable information as to who was who in ancient Palmyra. The brackets on the east side

Fig. 94 The Agora.

Fig. 95 Garstang's photograph
of the Agora before clearance
and excavation.

were reserved for senators, and it would appear from the slots in the wall inside the colonnade (Fig. 96) that they were either running short of space on the columns or that there were many more senators who needed honouring than there were pillars to accommodate their effigies. The treatment of the wall is a repetition of that in the Tariff Court. The Senators' entrance is fronted with a wider spacing in the colonnade and is emphasised by a pair of square columns to which are attached half columns. Whether it was made still more prominent by a feature above the cornice is impossible to say. The Gate was adorned with statues of the family of Septimius Severus whose wife was Syrian, being the daughter of the High Priest of Emesa (Homs).

The north portico was reserved for Roman and Palmyrene officials, the west for

Fig. 96 The east wall of the Agora.

Fig. 97 The Banqueting Chamber off the Agora.

soldiers, and the south for caravan leaders. In this way the pre-eminent of the city in all its important civic aspects were commemorated and their effigies left to gaze down on the hub of life to which they had greatly contributed. In all there were some two hundred statues in the Agora. The earliest inscription dates from the beginning of the reign of Hadrian (*c.* A.D. 71) indicating that it, and the Tariff Court with which it is schematically and architecturally linked, were begun about the middle of the first century A.D.

Today the complete circuit of walls is still standing to about 6 feet high except for some important parts of the east wall, two sections of the west and an impressive northern part with a trio of fine doors in it; there were originally eleven doors into the Agora. At the ends of the northern portico are water basins which are interestingly placed with their outer faces set across the corners.

The central space is cluttered by fewer stones than are usually to be found in such areas. There are a few neat rows of shafts and other pieces but one can appreciate the length and breadth of this enclosure. Desert scrub and succulents grow in the hard ground, softening the gold browns with welcome patches of green. There is a feeling of a sunken garden, abandoned and run wild, with delightful glimpses, if you lift your eyes, of the Colonnades which seem to appear abruptly out of the ground in a frenzy of perspectives. It is an area of warmth, enclosed yet spacious, that seems happy with its silence, not regretting the passing of the hubbub.

At the south-western angle a couple of pillars interrupt the wall and up four steps one enters a small BANQUETING CHAMBER (Fig. 97). There is an altar facing the door and vestiges of a shallow step round three sides of the room upon which would have been set the couches for the diners. These couches would have

Fig. 98 The peristyle of a building above the Agora.

been similar to the type we see on sarcophagi from tombs. In this triclinium were held certain of those ritual feasts to which it was a high honour to be invited. The cult image, or statue of the deity, in this shrine-cum-banqueting room has gone, but it would have stood in the niche over the altar as though presiding over the feast set in his honour. About shoulder height round the wall is a charming key or meander pattern string-course with parts of its deep carving still wonderfully crisp and clean. In its original state it was probably painted as well, which would have made it highly decorative.

Leaving the Agora by the small door in the north-eastern corner one is confronted by a steep bank of earth, the unexcavated area which holds the key to the layout of the area in front of the Senate portico. On the top of this bank stand six elaborately carved Corinthian pillars with reeded fluted shafts and rather un-

158

usually shaped brackets (Fig. 98). The quality of the workmanship is particularly fine with the thrown volutes of the capitals delicately cut. They are what remains of a peristyle court, the outlines of which are clearly traceable on the flagged floor. This peristyle was approached through a lobby with a door into the south portico of the Colonnade Street. The portal was a particularly grand affair with elaborate carved scroll brackets to the lintel, on which was a row of heads in high relief. It is now much battered and lying on the ground, but the heads still look strikingly well against a varying and waving palmette background.

The building was evidently of considerable importance judging by its sculptural qualities and properties. Also its location in an important part of the city close to the Senate and the Agora suggests that it served some civic or semi-state function. The majority of pillars which survive from private houses are devoid of brackets; only 'public' pillars seem to be so adorned. Inexplicably the westernmost bracket faces in the opposite direction from the others and certainly looks very odd. Only full excavation of the site will establish the date and purpose of this structure but it is nonetheless a beautiful row of columns and especially notable for the quality of its carving.

On the opposite side of the Colonnade Street, facing the double arch by the booths, are the remains of a NYMPHAEUM (Fig. 99). This was conceived on a very grand scale despite the rather cramped site. It terminated the vista down the transverse street from the Senate, and the central exedra would have echoed the double arch. Before the semi-circular water basin stood four tall columns on pedestals which were set forward of the main north colonnade of the Street. The central exedra in the rear wall between the two inner columns was flanked by a large niche on either side. It is probable that these were enriched with small pillars and 'Syrian' pediments. Since there are no corresponding pilasters on the wall, it may well be that the pillars were free-standing. By this means, they would have successfully masked the change in entablature levels, for the Street rises quite sharply at this point before reaching the Tetrapylon, and the remaining pillars of the Colonnade stand on a higher level. The solution to this problem is less successfully solved on the south side of the street where the wide span of the double arches could not mask the change in entablature levels. The impression is of one shoulder higher than the other.

The Nymphaeum was most richly ornamented with architectural detailing. This can be seen from the fragments lying on the ground which still retain their sharpness and boldness of relief. The detailing may seem a little crude but one has to remember that it would have been seen far above one's head where delicate touches would have been unseen in the bright sunlight.

Before going on to inspect the last columns of the Colonnade Street (Fig. 100), a small altar at the foot of the last pillar of the Nymphaeum should be noted.

Fig. 99 The remains of a Nymphaeum on the Colonnade Street, showing a fragment of its original cornice.

It is interesting to compare Fig. 100 with the photograph taken by Garstang in 1927 (Fig. 101) which shows the street in its unexcavated state. One can appreciate the enormous amount of clearance which has taken place in the last fifty years.

On two of the last eight columns of the southern portico are particularly interesting inscriptions. The second pillar supported a statue of Queen Zenobia, and the third, one of her husband, Odainat, who was murdered in A.D. 267. The bracket of Zenobia's pillar has gone and her name has been erased from the inscription; but the Roman destroyers at least spared Odainat's bracket. The inscriptions read:

Statue of Septimia Bat-Zabbai (the Greek translation of Zenobia), most Illustrious and Pious Queen; the excellent Septimii Zabda, general in chief, and Zabbai, military Governor of Tadmor, have raised it to their Lady, in the year 582 (A.D. 271) in August.

Statue of Septimius Odainat, King of Kings and Corrector of all the East, the excellent Septimii Zabda, general in chief, and Zabbai, military Governor of Tadmor, have raised it to their Lord, in the year 582 in August.

Fig. 100 The middle leg of the
Colonnade Street from near the
Tetrapylon.

Fig. 101 Garstang's 1920
photograph of the Colonnade
Street before clearance.

Odainat's statue was, therefore, posthumous. Exactly a year later, in August A.D. 272, Aurelian received the surrender of the city and took Zenobia into captivity. The Roman victors would have smashed her memorial and defaced her inscription but, remembering the stalwart support given to Valerian by Odainat, it is more than probable that they respected his effigy. The sight of Zenobia's memorial obliterated so soon after its erection, beside the untouched memorial to Odainat, would have been a salutary reminder to citizens of the rewards of loyalty and of treason.

The ground levels out, and the second change in the direction of the Street is marked and masked by the towering TETRAPYLON (Fig. 30). This consists of four independent pylons each of four enormous Corinthian columns of grey granite standing on a moulded square plinth at the four corners of a stepped platform. Each pylon had an identical entablature and within each stood a statue. For many years the fragments of the pillars, together with the pieces of the entablature, lay on the ground until the Department began restoring and re-erecting the monument in 1963. With the pieces of only one column remaining, the other fifteen had to be manufactured out of compounded concrete to match it in shape and colour. The reconstruction has created a much needed visual balance to the city which hitherto was far too heavily weighted at one end by the Monumental Arch and the great bulk of the Sanctuary of Bel. Now there is a point of equally impressive stature well away from the famous assemblage which provides a balance of interest. The re-erected Tetrapylon also provides a fine climax to the monuments of the central section of the Colonnade Street and then launches one on the excursion up the predominantly unexcavated western leg.

The Department has an enviable record of reinstatement of fallen monuments but it has to be questioned whether such wholesale faking of pillars as in the Tetrapylon is justified. Admittedly, the effect is marvellous and the matching excellently done, and the monument does serve once again the purpose for which it was designed. The balance between recreation and restoration is a fine one. But it can certainly be argued that such recreation as this invalidates the antique character of the monument for the visitor is not presented with the genuine article but a modern copy of it. There is another 'concrete' instance in Palmyra (see page 176) where the judgement of the Department is open to question, and whilst one can only have the greatest admiration for much of the work they do, some will hope that it will fall short of pastiche for effect's sake; a ruin is a ruin and no less interesting or fascinating for being so.

The second TRANSVERSE STREET which can be seen to the left is still substantially unexcavated. Its pillars erupt from the ground, brandishing their brackets, leading the eye away southwards to nowhere in particular. Tussocks of desert scrub deck the sandy earth and the area has a dream-like quality as the pillars stand, motionless and smiling, in the sunlit air.

PALMYRA TODAY

ZONE FOUR

Sanctuary of Baal Shamin, Honorific Column, The Basilica, Peristyle Houses, North Wall with Tower Tombs, Marona House Tomb, Streets, Upper Colonnade Street, and the Funerary Temple

The SANCTUARY OF BAAL SHAMIN (Fig. 102) is one of the very few complexes to have been thoroughly excavated. The Temple proper has changed little since Wood and Dawkins drew it (Fig. 103). The exploration party under Wiegand took due note of this building but it was the Swiss Archaeological mission under Professor Collart which finally established its plan and sorted out the complicated history of the site. Again, Garstang's photograph (Fig. 104) shows the state of the site before work began.

To the north of the Temple lies a spacious court surrounded on all four sides by colonnaded porticos. Inscriptions found on these columns show that a start was made in A.D. 23 although the west portico was redone in A.D. 257–8 during the reign of Odainat; an inscription mentions him as 'King of Palmyra'. The footings of the south portico are confused by the foundations of a Banqueting Chamber which, according to another inscription, was erected in A.D. 67 at the same time as the northern portico was begun. The Chamber was greatly modified when the Temple was built, for the south portico was open on both sides, giving a view from the courtyard through a forest of pillars to the side elevation of the cella.

It is interesting to note the difference in design of the capitals of the west portico from those on the three other sides. Those on the south, east and north are all of a nicely standard Corinthian type with clear detail and good undercutting (Fig. 105). The leaves, however, cannot be said to be acanthus in the true Hellenistic manner for there is a spikiness and rigidity about them which is accentuated by the face grooving on each 'leaf'. Despite this distinctly oriental interpretation of detail, they are unquestionably in the mode of the Hellenistic Corinthian capital. The same cannot be said of those on the west colonnade (Fig. 106). The outline and basic shape are still Corinthian but the detail is bulbous and solid with licking curves. The surrounding leaves are undecorated, being single lotus leaves with a strong vertical line which tucks under the top curve. The stemmed leaves, which support the miniature volutes, are treated in the same way and parallels for them can be found in Ptolemaic work. The whole influence here is Egyptian even though the volutes are recognisably a simplification of the Hellenistic form. This intrusion demonstrates that the Palmyrene trading and possibly political presence in Egypt led to strong cultural influences flowing into Palmyra. We have already seen this Ptolemaic influence in the architectural arrangement of the entrance door to the Temple of Bel.

163

Fig. 102 The Sanctuary of Baal Shamin.

Fig. 104 Garstang's view of the Temple.

Fig. 103 The drawing by Wood and Dawkins of the Temple of Baal Shamin.

Fig. 105 A Palmyrene Corinthian capital.

Fig. 106 A Romano-Egyptian capital.

165

Fig. 107 An aerial view of the Sanctuary of Baal Shamin.

Near the foundations of the Banqueting Chamber a section of a pillar can be seen with an effigy carved onto the shaft. This is a rare instance. The head is missing and the rest is sadly weathered, but the heavy folds of the clothes can clearly be distinguished. The tribe of the Bene Ma'azine had a long and important association with this Sanctuary, as a great number of inscriptions will attest, and it is tempting to muse on whether the stately figure on the column was one of their number.

The south courtyard was much smaller (Fig. 107) but was also surrounded by colonnaded porticos. The capitals are of the same Hellenistic, as opposed to Romano-Egyptian, pattern as those in the north courtyard. One of the columns of the north portico has been re-erected, and it carries an inscription in Palmyrene of A.D. 149 which gives us a date for the building of this part of the Sanctuary:

> These four columns with their upper parts and the ceiling were built by Hairan and Yamla, his brother, sons of Tama, son of Yamla; and were dedicated to Baal Shamin for their lives and those of their sons.

166

Fig. 108 The Temple of Baal Shamin.

Wedged between the two courtyards is the TEMPLE OF BAAL SHAMIN (Fig. 108). It has a handsome portico/pronaos of six columns, over the front four of which there was originally a pediment. The pillar to the left carries a bracket on which there is an inscription dated A.D. 130–31 which mentions Hadrian's visit to the city in A.D. 129, and that the temple was built under the aegis of Malé, son of Yarhai (and clerk to the Sanctuary) to the honour of Baal Shamin, Lord of Heaven and God of Fertility and of Storms and Rains.

167

The temple does not stand on a podium or krepis, but is approached direct from the ground by two steps. In this it is more consistent with oriental traditions than with Greek. The side and rear walls were adorned with pilasters. Pedimented windows were located high up on the two side walls. They are regular façades relying on their fine proportions and monumental scale for their effect rather than on dramatically original architectural ideas.

It is the treatment of the interior of the cella which is the surprise feature of the temple. Within one is faced with an elaborate adyton screen made up of an airy display of pillars, doors and shell-headed niches. The whole thing has been re-erected from fragments, the only disturbing feature being the putto which the German Archaeological Mission has inserted into one of the niches. The adyton would certainly not look out of place in a church by Bernini, Boromini or even by Hildebrandt or Fischer von Erlach, for it has real baroque qualities in the European sense of the word. And in that sense putti cavorting all over the place would be quite in keeping, but one must wonder whether the chubby child who blandishes from his niche in the Baal Shamin Temple is exactly appropriate.

There is a marvellous sense of movement with the deep central recess flanked by two rectangular sections. The carved detail is exceptionally rich, yet it is well under control and there is plenty of clean space to offset it. There is also great variety with the clustered fluted columns embracing plain ones in the same architectural rhythm and in the disposition of the openings. It is almost as though the central shrine was enmeshed in a fine net of architecture with space and light flowing in and out through the slender dance of stone. It is difficult to think of a precedent for this remarkable flight of imagination. Dr Lyttelton has pointed out that 'It is perhaps the only temple dating from classical antiquity known to have had a quasi-apsidal recess in the adyton.'*

Outside, in front of the portico, stands an altar with an inscription in both Palmyrene and Greek dating from A.D. 115.

Like the Temple of Bel, the Baal Shamin was converted into a church during the Byzantine period. The entrance was then moved to the west—probably occasioning the destruction of the adyton screen—with a new mud-brick portico on that end, built over an old graveyard. The Bishop of Palmyra, Marinus, was one of the signatories of the Council of Nicaea, and so we have proof of the presence of Christians in Palmyra in A.D. 325. In fact it is almost certain that they were there as early as a century before.

The Temple has, however, been skilfully restored to its original arrangement and is one of the best preserved of all the monuments of the city. In many ways it is one of the most attractive.

* *Baroque Architecture in Classical Antiquity.*

To the north of the Sanctuary stands the shabby and dingy Zenobia Hotel with its uninteresting façade staring blindly, like a monstrous platitude, over the ruins.

To the east, across the road which leads to the new town, stands a tall HON-ORIFIC COLUMN. This was raised by the Senate and the people and carried a bronze statue of the dedicatee. There are four such isolated columns in Palmyra, but when the whole site has been systematically examined—particularly the area to the south of the so-called Zenobia wall—it may be revealed that there were many more of this type of monument. Honouring of notable citizens was an unashamed passion of the Palmyrenes: it is almost as though there were as many people upon pedestals as there were on the ground, as many reminders as reminded, past and present lending animation to each other. It was one way of telling the citizenry that the city depended on them. The very psychology of public recognition gives a marvellous insight into the social thinking and drive of Palmyrene society.

Beyond the Honorific Column stretches a broad band of green, date orchards, sunken and mud-brick walled, which shield the new town from the old.

Near the NORTH GATE, through which the new road passes, are the remains of a large complex of rectangular buildings, the remains of which suggest barracks.

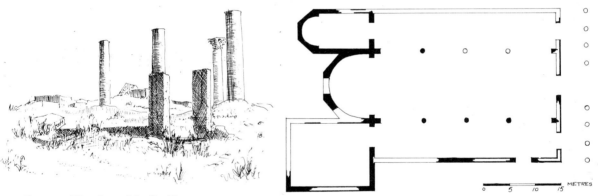

Fig. 109 The plan of the Basilica.

There are two, possibly three, Christian Basilicas in Palmyra. The unexcavated remains of one lie to the north of the hotel and present little for the visitor to examine. However, a short distance to the west of the Sanctuary of Baal Shamin there is a low mound from which a handful of columns project. The plan of this BASILICA is still quite clear (Fig. 109) showing a typical Byzantine church of moderate size. The interior was divided by two rows of columns into a nave and two aisles. The central nave terminated at the east end in a broad apse, over which there was originally an arch, whilst the aisles ended in doors giving into small chambers. One was probably a baptistry or a shrine housing the relics of a saint.

Fig. 110 The peristyles of two houses in the
north-west quarter of the city.

The west door was sheltered by a porch or Narthex with six columns standing on steps.

Even though the site has not been excavated it can be seen that the plan has numerous parallels with Byzantine and Early Christian churches right across the eastern Mediterranean, even as far as in Rome herself. No definite date can yet be put on the building—this can only come with excavation—but it falls into the sixth-century bracket, possibly a part of the Justinian period. What is also clear is that it was purpose built and not an adaptation of an earlier structure. Material from other buildings might well have been re-used here but it was built with precision and a sense of balance.

To the west of the Basilica stand the peristyles (Fig. 110) of two houses. These would have formed the central courtyards of houses of prosperous citizens. One is almost complete (Fig. 111), a square of sixteen columns standing strangely alone and unrelated, with the outlines of walls upon the ground. During the heyday of Palmyra there must have been many PERISTYLE HOUSES, mostly dating from the second century when private individuals were expressing their unbounded optimism and material well-being in a fine house for themselves.

A pattern of long, straight and narrow STREETS can be seen clearly on the

Fig. 111 The peristyle of a house of a wealthy
Palmyrene which should be compared with Fig. 2.

rough and stony ground (see page 28), leading away to the north from the Upper
Colonnade Street. This appears to have been a residential part of the town and,
judging from the size and scale of the buildings, to have been an aristocratic or at
least wealthy quarter. Today, it remains one of the areas untouched by excavators
and is, in consequence, much as it was in the eighteenth-century days of Wood and
Dawkins. Occasionally pillars sprout from the scrub, odd abandoned slabs of
stone, some with intricate carving upon them, others plain and with no identity, lie
scattered amid the weeds. There is a stark silence in the air, the white light dancing
distractingly. In the evening the mood softens, golden melancholy floods coolly
over everything, colours richen and contrasts soften. Through this wash of falling
light one wanders slowly, for haste would seem a sacrilege.

A short distance beyond this area lies the NORTH WALL which, like that in the
south, is believed to have been part of Zenobia's fortification of the city. It is
punctuated with towers every 37 metres. Justinian made every fourth tower
semi-circular except at the western end of the wall, where tower tombs were used
as bastions. The exact date of the wall is still uncertain.

Fig. 112 The Marona house tomb.

To the north of the city wall stands the large MARONA HOUSE TOMB (Fig. 112). It was re-erected by the Department in 1946 after partial collapse. Originally built in March A.D. 236 by Julius Arlius Marona, it was designed to serve as a mausoleum for himself and his family. From a series of bas-reliefs found when the monument was re-erected it appears that the family were merchants with wide maritime ramifications, for one particular relief shows a Palmyrene shipowner standing by his ship. The building is almost square with plain dressed stone walls with pilasters at all four corners and a fully articulated entablature. The large portal was on the west side and this led into the usual interior with walls of niches or loculi for the bodies. There is likely to have been a statuary group of Julius

Fig. 113 The Upper Colonnade Street.

Marona with his family, lounging sedately and in splendour on a couch. Unfortunately the tomb was turned into a house at a later stage when mud-brick vaults were inserted, destroying the internal plan. The monument is also known as the Kasr el Hayye (Palace of the Serpent) because the capital of the south-eastern pilaster has a snake carved into the decorative detail. The architectural ornament is in the usual lush Palmyrene manner but here there is a marked restraint about it.

Of the UPPER COLONNADE STREET, from the Tetrapylon to the Funerary Temple, little has been excavated (Fig. 113). A few trenches have been put down, revealing one or two important features but the majority of the colonnades are still very broken, and in consequence highly romantic. The most important single

Fig. 114 An exedra on the Upper Colonnade Street.

thing to have come to light is a large EXEDRA—possibly another Nymphaeum—on the south side just past the Tetrapylon (Fig. 114). Its plan is elaborate with a wide central apse flanked on either side by smaller ones. Massive corner pilasters framed the central opening and presumably carried an arch, whilst the whole feature was carried on a low plinth which describes the full half circle. This plinth stops under the return of the pilasters and the side apses are treated architecturally as separate entities. Next to the side apses are engaged half columns on their own plinths which would have created a self-contained feeling and added a sense of solidity to the massive central opening. The great central apse was enriched with a series of paired miniature columns, the alternating intercolumnations being crowned with the usual 'Syrian' pediments. The treatment would then have been more of a surface screen and one is reminded of the inner wall of the Propylaea of the Sanctuary of Bel where similar 'blind' architectural screens are such a grand feature of the surface decoration. In front of the Exedra stood four fluted columns on the same alignment as the Colonnade of the street which were probably bridged by an entablature, possibly with a segmental arch over the central opening much in the manner of the Propylaea of the Sanctuary of Bel. This, however, is conjectural as the area round has not been cleared and there

Fig. 115 The Upper Colonnade Street.

are insufficient fragments upon which to base a firm hypothesis. The whole feature must have been, nonetheless, very grand and would have been another of those breaks in a long colonnade which were designed to relieve any sense of monotony.

Beyond the Exedra there are just pillars, pillars and yet more pillars. They stand, rearing up from the ground, or lie pathetically where they have fallen, broken into pieces, with scrub, grasses and weeds playing about them. Sections of entablature lunge up from the earth at crazy angles or lie in hapless piles at the feet of the columns which once carried them so high. There is a marvellous sense of ruin, untouched by science when every stone is marshalled into order. The experience which Rose Macaulay has called 'pleasure in ruins' can here be enjoyed to the full (Fig. 115).

Very close to the Funerary Temple a part of the north portico has been cleared, revealing a strong stone wall. This ends in a fantastic pile of huge stones with many richly carved architectural details among it. Clearly this is a collapsed House Tomb of the Marona type but possibly rather more richly ornamented. This must surely be a target for the restorers of the Department in future years.

Fig. 116 The pillars at the end of the Upper Colonnade Street showing the rise in levels of the pillar bases.

Fig. 117 A conjectural reconstruction of an arch which terminated the Upper Colonnade Street, through which can be seen the Funerary Temple. Note the rise in the levels of the bases of the pillars.

Beside this pile the Upper Colonnade Street comes to a halt in an interesting way (Fig. 116). It will be noticed that the shaft of the last pillar on each side of the road is shorter than the others, with its base considerably above its neighbours. Despite the severe erosion, it would appear that the base of the pilaster which carries the end of the colonnade was higher still. From this pilaster project fragments of a wall. There is an immense amount of fallen masonry heaped up about the place, and to try and make sense of it is not at present possible. There are, however, indications that the street was terminated by a large arch approached up a stepped ramp, through which would have been framed the portico of the Funerary Temple (Fig. 117).

The FUNERARY TEMPLE (Fig. 118) is really a particularly sumptuous house tomb which should properly be called 'Temple Tombs'. Until recently only the portico remained standing, see Garstang's photograph (Fig. 119), but the Department has re-erected the south and west walls, thus creating a more substantial visual effect at the end of the vista up the Colonnade Street. It has also made it much easier to appreciate the scale of the monument. A considerable amount of smoothed concrete had to be used to replace seriously eroded stone, which is fair

Fig. 118 The Funerary Temple.

Fig. 119 Garstang's photograph
of the Funerary Temple before the
rear and one of the side walls were
reconstructed.

enough for it has been done tactfully. But it is in the recreation of the crypt beneath the present floor that one must disagree with what here amounts to concrete mania. Admittedly the outlines of the original arrangement are now shown, but the concrete is used wholesale so that the effect is bogus. One can only lament that the Department could not have left well alone and been content with reinstating the walls, leaving the vault open to view in its fragmentary state.

The monument dates from the third century. Wiegand proposed a conjectural scheme for the interior, based to a great extent on the layout of the vault (Fig. 120). Corinthian pilasters, standing on plinths, were ranged round the walls with loculi stacked between them. The closing-stones of the loculi carried a portrait relief of the 'inmate'—in the fullness of time providing a veritable family portrait gallery. The pilasters reached only half-way up the walls and carried a boldly sculptured entablature, the frieze of which is believed to have been of the palm-tree pattern. Above the entablature, the upper parts of the walls were embellished with broad pillared and pedimented niches in which were housed statuary groups. The central space was dominated by a two-storey pylon of four columns supporting a square entablature at both levels. This acted as a shrine for the founder of the tomb. The whole impression would have been overwhelming, both architecturally and emotionally. All that architecture thundering about you and all those faces of the past gazing stonily down with the central statue sitting as though in judgement on your intrusion, would have been oppressive. This is a western European reaction to ancestor worship but it is important to realise that for the Palmyrenes things were different. To be surrounded by one's own dead gave you a family 'hot line' to the gods. Nepotism beyond the grave is quite an achievement.

The temple is raised on a low plinth with a short flight of steps rising to the centre of the portico. The vine-scroll carving of the pilasters which catch the returns of the portico is particularly noteworthy. This type of ornament is common in Palmyra but it is interesting to see it *in situ* on a small scale monument. It is often found in the late Graeco-Roman world, a notable example being in the Severan Basilica at Leptis Magna, but there the degree of undercutting is very marked, creating almost a traceried effect, whereas in Palmyra the decorative detail is always treated as surface ornament. The proportions of the Funerary Temple are particularly happy and there is a nobility about it with strong muscular lines and precise articulation.

Fig. 120 Reconstruction of the interior
of the Funerary Temple, based on
Wiegand's plans and elevations.

PALMYRA

The Third Transverse Street, the Oval Piazza and Damascus Gate, the Temple of Allat, Diocletian's Camp and the West Walls

Running south from the Funerary Temple is another colonnaded street dating from the second century. It is 22 metres wide, much wider than the main Colonnade Street. This led to an oval piazza and the Damascus Gate. Most of the pillars have fallen but the line of the street is still clear. A great number of inscriptions have come to light, the most important of which records the setting up of six columns of the portico in A.D. 129 to the honour of the deities Shams, Allat and Rahm. These gods are of Arab origin. The sun god Sham or Shamash was the son of the moon god Sin, who was deeply rooted in Mesopotamian culture, and was the lord of knowledge by whom the passing of the months was governed. It is interesting that Shamash was only the son of the moon god for elsewhere the sun is accorded the greater position as the giver of life. But in the east it is only in the morning when the sun chases away the shadows in which evil and terror can lurk that he is regarded as benign. Later in the day he can scorch, destroy and kill. Then the sun becomes Nergal, the god of the nether regions, peopled with the victims of suffering. Shamash, however, was regarded primarily as the god of justice, a natural concomitant to his father's patronage of knowledge and wisdom.

Rahm is mentioned in southern and northern Arabian texts as the god of mercy, a religious concept which the Abbé Starcky has pointed out plays an important part in Semitic religions. In Palmyra one occasionally finds the attribute 'to Him whose name is blessed for ever' followed by the credit 'the kind, the merciful and the compassionate', which points to the pre-Moslem concepts of Islam. The Prophet Mohammed probably adopted and adapted much of the existing Arabian religious vocabulary.

The monotheistic theme occurs in the last dedicatee, Allat, for her name is the feminine of Allah who was invoked in northern Arabia at that time as Ilah, simply meaning 'God'. The cult of Ilah is exceedingly old and by inference raises the problem of monotheism amongst nomadic Arab tribes long before the advent of Islam. Allat (Ishtar in Mesopotamian culture) was the divine personification of the planet Venus, goddess both of love and of destruction. The Arab historian Ibn al Kelbi recounts her worship in Arabia. Her special province was fertility and reproduction, though her penchant for destruction shows her as a very ambivalent character. For a goddess of love she was without a spark of compassion; she was fickle, insatiable and cruel, gobbling up her numerous lovers, even destroying the young god of the harvest, Tammuz, in her passion—over whom she then lamented

Fig. 121 The ruins of the Temple of Allat.

with almost operatic intensity. She was greatly feared as well as venerated: well was she named the 'Morning Star' whom the Greeks called 'Hesperos', the destroyer.

The first century TEMPLE OF ALLAT lay a short distance to the west of the Damascus Colonnade Street and its ruins (Fig. 121) are clearly distinguishable. All that remains is the doorway, presumably to the cella or to the Temenos, and a clutch of fluted Corinthian columns, for the most part lying on the ground. The doorway, now very badly weathered, is portrayed on the left of Wood and

Fig. 123 The remains of the Oval Piazza.

Fig. 122 The drawing by Wood and Dawkins of the Temple of Allat and the Camp of Diocletian.

Fig. 124 Reconstruction of the Oval Piazza and the Damascus Gate.

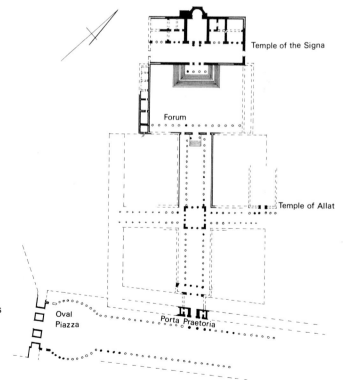

Temple of the Signa

Forum

Temple of Allat

Oval Piazza

Porta Praetoria

Fig. 125 The plan of Diocletian's Camp (based on the plan published by Professor Michalowski).

0 10 20 30 40 50 METRES

Dawkins' picture of the so-called Diocletian's Camp (Fig. 122). There is little to suggest the residential buildings which are believed to have surrounded the temple during the first century, though this may not be altogether surprising because the site was overtaken by the Diocletian's Camp complex during the turn of the second century when the whole area assumed a much more grandiose character. The layout of the Damascus Colonnade Street and the final development of the Camp site must have largely obliterated the original character of the district.

The Damascus Colonnade Street ends in a shallow OVAL PIAZZA of which only a handful of bracketed Corinthian pillars remain today (Fig. 123). There are parallels for this piece of baroque town planning in other Graeco-Roman cities, notably the huge Forum at Jerash in Jordan, but here the oval was treated as an integral part of the Damascus Gate. The southern ends of the oval were joined to the gate by arches which would probably have been repeated in the façade itself. On entering the city one would have the impression of sweeping, welcoming arms of pillars. The approach from the street would have been most dramatic with the gate being emphasised by the colonnades suddenly swelling out round the piazza and then swinging in to grasp the flanks of the façade (Fig. 124). This is another example of the imaginative planning where an unashamed striving for effect was adopted. Pleasure was taken in devising visual excitement.

To the west of the Damascus Street lies one of the most important archaeological sites in the whole of Palmyra. This is the so-called CAMP OF DIOCLETIAN. It has been the subject of examination by the Polish Archaeological Mission since 1959, under the direction of Professor K. Michalowski. Examination of the evidence will go on for a few years yet but enough has been studied and published for an outline to be drawn.

The western district which includes the Camp is indisputably one of the oldest urban centres in Palmyra. Ruins of dwellings with walls of the polygonal type dating from the turn of the first century have been uncovered together with an honorific column with a dedication dated A.D. 64—one of the earliest periods in the city's development. The whole of this district was probably dominated by the predecessor of what is now referred to as the Temple of the Signa, with the nearby Temple of Allat as the principal religious sanctuary in the area. The so-called Forum before the Temple of the Signa certainly existed before the development we see today, and it is probable that, being approached by a staircase, it constituted a kind of High Place in the Semitic usage: the Polish excavations found a great number of altars dedicated to the 'Nameless god'.

The adaptation of a major portion of this western sector as a Roman military camp was undertaken at the instigation of Sosianus Hierocles, whom we have already met as the driving force behind the development of the Diocletian Baths.

The Camp was entered from the Damascus Colonnade Street some 90 metres

Fig. 126 Reconstruction of the Tetrapylon in Diocletian's Camp.

short of the Gate, through a triple arched entrance called the *Porta Praetoria*, in the western street portico. This replaced an earlier structure. It was the entrance to the CASTRA ROMANA (Fig. 125), and westwards from it led a wide thoroughfare, the *Via Principalis* of the Camp, lined with porticos. This and the street which crossed it were part of the previous development of the area before Hierocles initiated the district's conversion into a fortified Roman Camp. Where the *Via Principalis* crossed the *Via Praetoria*, at right angles, Hierocles constructed a massive tetrapylon in the form of a quadrapartite arch (Fig. 126). The colonnades of the *Via Praetoria* joined the tetrapylon on the outer corners of the wall whereas those of the *Via Principalis* abutted on the intercolumnation in a most awkward way. This must have been one of the least happy architectural solutions to have come out of Palmyra, a city remarkable for the facility of its town planning and architectural arrangements.

Beyond this there is a further length of the *Via Principalis* which begins to rise up the gentle slope of the western hill. The street culminates in a kind of propylaea, also redeveloped under the aegis of Sosianus Hierocles. This led up a monumental

Fig. 127 The steps of the Temple of the Signa.

flight of steps into the Square of the Altars. The square was a miniature Forum acting as a prelude to the climax of the military Camp, the TEMPLE OF THE SIGNA or Temple of the Standards. This stood on a high podium and was fronted by a tall portico of four monolithic Corinthian columns on a flight of sixteen steps which even today seem to flood down towards one (Fig. 127). The relationship between portico and steps is dramatic; the effect would have been greatly enhanced when related to the enclosed Forum in which it stood (Fig. 128). One would have looked up this billowing spate of steps to the deeply projecting portico. Behind this loomed the plain, unrelieved wall of the Temple with its tiled roof. One's whole attention was concentrated on the doors to the Temple.

Within was the Holy of Holies, remote and detached, approached only up that awesome staircase. It lay across a large hall set transversely, 60 metres long and 12 metres wide, with the richly decorated entrance to the cella immediately opposite. Over the portal was the inscription naming Sosianus Hierocles as builder of the Camp of Diocletian. On either side of the central cella, the Holy of Holies, were other chambers or groups of chambers approached through pillared entrances. As Professor Michalowski has pointed out, the Temple of the Signa really only refers

186

Fig. 128 Reconstruction of the Temple of the Signa.

Fig. 129 The Sanctuary of the Signa.

to 'the central part of the structure (Fig. 129) where the military insignia were kept. This might have served as the praetorium of the Roman Camp.'* This central part, the cella, ends in a bold apse with the arch supported on blind pilasters (pilasters where the shafts are not articulated from the wall surface, but still have capitals and bases) with richly carved capitals. There was not a full entablature, only a deep stepped architrave which swept back round the apse. The same moulding was used as a hooding for the arch. The walls were adorned with niches, pillared and pedimented in the usual Palmyrene way with the cornice moulding extending as a string course round the apse, linking the three niches. The floor of the apse was set above the level of the rest of the cella, thus forming a sort of rostrum. The only light would have been from torches and lamps and such fitful gloom as would have percolated in through the entrance portal and lunette windows placed high up in the large hall. Architecture serves a purpose, a human need, and to be aware of the emotions it was intended to stir is to grasp the nature of its purpose. Imagine a recruit being taken from parade in the Forum, up those steps—possibly alone or with one or two 'sponsors'—and vanishing from sight beneath the portico into the silent temple. In the gloom of the cella he takes his oath amid the flickering lamps and with the standards winking gold, casting strange hovering shadows on the wall of the apse before him. A moment of supreme isolation and yet one which wrapped him in a world greater than his own. The Roman world knew how to impress, how to stir violent emotion.

Krencker, in his analysis of the structure as a whole, has pointed out comparisons between the Palmyra Temple of the Signa and the chapels of the Signa in other Roman Camps, notably the one at Lambaesis in North Africa where the similarity is most striking.

On both sides of the square in front of the Forum the excavators found a series of chambers, probably military storerooms, some of which were even furnished with sanitary installations.

The debate still rages about the use to which this complex was originally put, that is, before it was changed into a Roman military camp. More particularly, the character and function of the Temple of the Signa is questioned. Was it a temple, a palace, a stately municipal building or what? This will remain open to discussion for many years to come, and even the publication of the final excavation report of the Polish Expedition is unlikely to resolve it finally, for there will almost inevitably be different interpretations of the evidence. One fact remains established, that as Professor Michalowski has put it, 'on the orders of Sosianus Hierocles, the building was substantially modified and extended, with blocks originating from older structures serving as material'.† It can also be fairly stated that the area was

* Michalowski, *Palmyra*.   † Ibid.

Fig. 130 The view over the ruined city from above Diocletian's Camp.

turned into a military camp. The Hierocles inscription specifically states:

> Camp was founded by the Emperors Diocletian and Maximian and the Caesars Constantius and Maximianus ... Sosianus Hierocles governor of the province having supervised (the work) ...

Certainly by the middle of the second century the streets which became the *Via*

189

Praetoria and *Via Principalis* were already in existence, as was a propylaea leading to the Square of the Altars—later to become the Forum of the Roman Camp. By any standards this was a monumental layout and this fact, together with cross analysis of architectural details, has led the French scholar, Schlumberger, to suggest that it was the palace of the fabulous Queen Zenobia. It is tempting to assign everything to Zenobia but the Abbé Starcky has emphasised 'the supposition that it may have been a palace is not to be dismissed'. Schlumberger proposes a date during the reign of Odainat and Zenobia—the sculptural detail is remarkably close to that of the Funerary Temple—and suggests that despite the long Latin Hierocles inscription, the building would have only been restored and adapted to a new, military purpose under Diocletian, the inscription being inserted into an already existing fabric. Whatever the outcome, it is beyond question that the site was, even before the Hierocles developments, of considerable importance and would have provided a visual counterweight to balance the great bulk of the Sanctuary of Bel at the other end of the city.

One final consideration of this site is the possible influence its layout had on the famous Ummayyad desert castles. It has long been accepted that their plan is basically that of a Roman Camp—Anjar in the Bekka in Lebanon is a classic example of an Ummayyad town and Mashatta a fort. The Ummayyad dynasty was centred on Damascus and was therefore at the vortex of all the various cultural forces which whirled about the Levant and its hinterland after the fall of the Roman Empire and later retreat of the Byzantines.

Behind the Camp rises an abrupt hill which dominates the western part of the city. The north city wall is very conspicuous as it climbs up the side of the slope to be greeted by the remains of the south wall on the top. It is worth climbing the hill (walk up by the north wall because the going is easier) for the view back over the city is remarkably fine (Fig. 130). The best time is early evening when the sun is going down, casting long shadows. Below you are the Polish excavations of Diocletian's Camp with their layout looking a lot clearer and more intelligible than when you are on site. To the left is the Funerary Temple from which the Colonnade Street sweeps out across the flat, its scattered stands of pillars motionless and sentinel. Away in the distance the Tetrapylon, now looking diminutive, is caught up in the jumble of pillars with the Monumental Arch adding to the visual confusion. Beyond and detached, floats the huge bulk of the Sanctuary of Bel. Long strips of green are painted across the distances before the view tips towards the hazy blue horizon in shades of buff, grey and gold. The scrub and grasses which clothe the ground of the city are turned to that dark, rich green against which the golden pillars and littered stones stand out with delightful clarity and harmony. Consider this landscape, populated now by pillars, for what you are looking at is the site of the city. Those bare acres were once crowded with dwellings and

Fig. 131 The Valley of Tombs.

humanity, pulsating with life. All this has long gone. What remains is there to remind us of what has vanished. It is a sobering thought, but there is comfort in the knowledge that this was very much a city of the living, for as one turns and faces west and sees the Valley of Tombs with its stark sentinel towers against the setting sun, one is faced with a city of the dead (Fig. 131).

Fig. 132 Wood and Dawkins' drawing of the Tower Tomb of Kithoth.

ZONE SIX

The Valley of Tombs, Ain Efqa, The South-west Necropolis, The South-east Necropolis, Walls

Even though tower tombs are such a distinctive feature of Palmyra, they were not the only type of mausoleum used. There are also hypogea (underground galleries), house or temple tombs (the Marona House Tomb and the Funerary Temple have already been discussed and are good examples) and a combination of tower cum hypogeum. The tower tombs are the oldest type and can be dated from as early as the Hellenistic period. The earliest ones were built of roughly and irregularly shaped blocks of stone with small infill (Fig. 1). There are similarities in this building technique with Archaic Greek work known as 'polygonal' but it would be incautious to suggest any direct influence. The steeply stepped base upon which the tower usually stands was always a feature, and again one is reminded of the krepidoma of a Greek temple. Internally there were several floors reached by a narrow staircase. On each landing were loculi, into which the bodies of the dead were placed and which were then sealed with a sculptural portrait of the deceased. The larger, later, towers were not only lavishly decorated but were spacious enough to hold up to four hundred corpses. The early ones, however, were rather more modest. Because of the random nature of the laying of the stones, these 'polygonal' stone towers have survived none too well and are, in the main, now only stumps. As time passed the cutting of the stones became more regular and thus the construction stronger.

Descending the hill behind Diocletian's Camp one comes to the TOWER TOMB OF KITHOTH, son of Thaimarsu, which is known locally as the Kasr el Madrus (Fig. 1 and extreme right of Fig. 132). This is a good example of that stage of development where the blocks are beginning to be made rather more regular whilst remaining distinctly polygonal. It has a strong four-stepped base in which is set the entrance to the inner chamber. The main point of interest is the fine sculptural funerary group still *in situ* in the arched recess high up on the wall. Usually these groups are placed over the door. The arch is decorated with bold, not very subtle, intertwining vine decoration and does not appear to have been supported by pilasters as suggested in the Wood and Dawkins drawing. The sill on which the composition rested has certainly vanished. Within the arch is the funerary group with the 'head of the family' lying on a couch surrounded by his immediate kin. Although heads are missing, this is a well preserved piece and the draperies are particularly attractive. Part of the inscription below the couch has also vanished—taking the right leg of the couch with it. This couch is typical, a cloth-wrapped mattress on a frame, the legs of which one suspects were turned on a lathe. This style of furniture occurs frequently in funerary sculpture and is certainly derived from domestic examples, which would have been found in well-to-do private houses in the city.

Across the valley is a line of tower tombs (Fig. 133) which cling to the steep sides of a low hill called Umm el Belquis. The tall one on the right-hand side is the famous TOWER TOMB OF IAMLICHU (Fig. 134). It dates from A.D. 83 and carries an inscription below the elaborate niche high up on the entrance wall:

Iamlichu, son of Mokimu Akalisch, son of Maliku, son of Belakab, son of Mike, son of Maththa, Councillor of Tadmor ...

The entrance door was grandly decorated with a wide architrave and surmounted by a richly sculptured pediment on brackets. The niche above is thrown forward on two corbels carved as winged victories. On these would have originally been free standing pillars supporting an entablature and pediment, within which would have stood the funerary group. The tower is four storeys high and is capped by a fine carved cornice. The stone blocks are well dressed to a regular shape and there is a clear, clean-cut appearance which makes the doorway and projecting niche particularly prominent. Its elevated position on the slope of Umm el Belquis gives it a commanding presence and affords it a fine view back towards the city.

Fig. 133 Tower Tombs on the flank of Umm el Belquis.

The chief glory of the Iamlichu tower tomb is its interior (Fig. 135) which was skilfully and tactfully restored by the Department in 1963. The walls are lined with Corinthian pilasters, between which were set tiers of loculi, the rich cornice still carrying good traces of the original colouring. The ceiling is a complex pattern of diamond and triangular shaped coffers between bold, grooved straps: the coffers contained portrait busts but these are now very much decayed. The ground floor is strongly architectural but is in no way overpowering. The entrance to the upper storeys is at the back via a much less pretentious doorway. It is interesting to note that remains of cloth were found in this tomb, in particular pieces of Chinese silk (see page 31).

The other tower tombs on this flank can all be named according to the families which built them. It sounds like a roll-call of the 'top brass' of Palmyra. Next to the

Fig. 134 The Tower Tomb of Iamlichu.

Fig. 135 The interior of the main chamber of the Tower Tomb of Iamlichu by L.–F. Cassas.

Iamlichu is the BANAI, LAASCHA and ARRAUM TOMB, sons of Thaimischa, son of Banai called Adona, then the TOMB OF HAIRAN, son of Belsuri, son of Gaddarso, the TOMBS OF SABEIS, OF ELASCHA, OF JULIUS AURELIUS BOLMA, son of Zabdibol, and so on.

In their day, before the so-called Zenobia Wall was built, these tombs would have been very close to the southern tip of the city. Now they stand well back, curiously remote and detached, as though they have crept secretly out of the valley of the dead to gaze wistfully at the ruins of the city of the living.

Below, in the valley, the pebble path winds its white way westwards, slowly ascending the passage of the watercourse. All about are the shattered stumps of tower and house tombs. After a while one mound of rubble (Fig. 136) begins to look like the next but it is worth exploring those tombs from which the cascades of

Fig. 136 Collapsed tower tombs.

rubble have been cleared. In many cases there are interesting fragments of architectural sculpture to be seen as well as some clearly visible internal arrangements.

Eventually the path comes onto a level area far up the valley on which there is an important group of monuments. The area is wide open to the skies with the steep hillsides set well back and with a splendid view of the Ottoman Castle perched upon its eminence far away to the north-east. The scene is dominated by the huge TOWER TOMB OF ELAHBEL (Fig. 137), son of Maani, which was completed in A.D. 103. The tower has been restored but the Wood and Dawkins engraving and old photographs show that it was in a remarkable state of preservation even before the Department set to work. It is named after one of the four founders of the tomb, Elahbel, Shaqai, Moqimo and Maani, all sons of Maani, a family prominent in

Fig. 137 The Tower Tomb of Elahbel.

Fig. 138 The interior of the main chamber of the
Tower Tomb of Elahbel by L.–F. Cassas.

Palmyrene civic affairs and one responsible for much effort towards the construction of the Temple of Nebo.

The tower is raised on a high podium in which, on the south side is a handsome
door with the lintel of the architrave hanging in a seemingly unsupported way. To
either side of it are worn scroll brackets which supported the ends of the elaborately carved cornice. The original doors, now replaced with an iron grill gate,
would have been massive stone slabs, probably carved with the shallow coffer
pattern so frequently found in Palmyrene tombs.

Above the podium are the familiar three steps before the walls rise to a beautifully scaled cornice. Except for small lancet windows lodged in the spacing of the
stones, the walls are quite unadorned except for the south which has a bilingual
inscription plaque and an arched niche. The figures from this arch have long

197

vanished—they are even missing in the Wood and Dawkins drawing—but the couch upon which the principal member would have lain is preserved. The hooding of the arch was carved with boldly chiselled motifs which even today stand out in high relief. On the northern side there is also a door, placed low in the podium which led down into a vault beneath.

The interior is particularly spectacular, vying with the Iamlichu Tower Tomb in its splendour (Fig. 138). Here again there are tall Corinthian pilasters against the walls with tiers of loculi between them. Over the door is a bust of the *curator* of the tomb who was Elahbel's son. There are several sculptural panels still *in situ*, which gives an added interest to the architectural composition. The ceiling is very fine, a straight geometric set of small coffers containing rosettes, with some larger coffers in which are set portrait busts. Traces of the original colouring also remain and indicate how brilliant this interior must have been. The central section of the ceiling has fallen and fortunately no attempt has been made to replace it with a concrete imitation. To the left, on entering, is a narrow staircase which leads to the upper floors which were also appointed with loculi. From the roof there is a magnificent view back down the Valley of Tombs with the pillar forest of the city stretched across the horizon.

Just beyond the Elahbel Tower Tomb is the core of another tower tomb known locally as the Kasr el Tanwill, but properly as the TOWER TOMB OF ATHENATHAU. It rises like a roughened spire and is a landmark because of its present conical shape. It may have been the sight of this which so raised Dr Halifax's hopes of finding the remains of Christian churches. Close inspection reveals the remains of loculi in its tapering core, around which winds a narrow staircase. Most of the outer wall has long since collapsed and vanished.

A short distance beyond this are the remains of a fine house tomb with a great many architectural fragments still to be seen (Fig. 139). This was excavated by Ingholt in 1928 and is known as the Kasr el Abjad.

In this vicinity are the remains of a number of hypogea, or underground galleries, hewn into the rock on a cruciform plan or forming the letter 'T'. The rock in Palmyra is so perishable that it was found necessary to separate the individual loculi with terracotta slabs. This hypogeum type of tomb became common in Palmyra in the first half of the second century A.D.; in fact the type is encountered most frequently, its number exceeding those of tower tombs or house tombs.

In the Valley of Tombs the best known hypogea are those of Bolbarakh (A.D. 139), Nurbel (A.D. 134), Salamallath (A.D. 147) and pre-eminently, the Yarhai (A.D. 108). The HYPOGEUM OF THE YARHAI lies close to the Elahbel Tower Tomb but there is little enough today to be seen on the site. Due to the nature of the rock the whole interior was faced with hard limestone designed as a complicated, almost baroque, composition (Fig. 140) (see page 210). This is an important work

Fig. 139 Architectural fragments in a ruined house tomb. Note the crispness of the detail, particularly of the blind fluting.

Fig. 140 Part of the interior of the Yarhai Hypogeum as rebuilt in the crypt of the Damascus Museum, showing portrait sculptures closing the loculi in which the depicted deceased were placed. See also Fig. 4.

and has been transported to the Damascus Museum and partially reconstructed there in a specially prepared crypt. In consequence the natural rock has crumbled and the site of the tomb is now a mess. To get the real impact of the almost bizarre grandeur of the architectural treatment, one has to visit the Damascus Museum. Even there, unfortunately, only a part of the whole was re-erected, so one does not get the full impression of the hypogeum with its fascinating spatial relationships.

Bearing in mind that funeral ceremonies and access were as important as accommodating the dead, it was the Polish team who succeeded in unravelling the spatial layout employed in hypogea. They also established that tower tombs of the early years of the first century A.D. were not isolated monuments but were raised above a hypogeum complex. This enables archaeologists now to locate hypogea of the period with far greater ease. An additional aid, to which attention was drawn by D. P. Crouch in a recent article,* was that of aerial photography in which 'Many underground tombs at Palmyra may be located by their light-toned marks on aerial photographs.'

In these tower-cum-hypogeum tombs the main door does not lead into a grand ground floor chamber such as in the Iamlichu Tower Tomb, but gives direct onto a flight of steps descending abruptly and steeply into a hypogeum. There is a very good example of this near the Elahbel Tower Tomb where, amid a group of shattered stumps and holes in the ground, the doorway of Tower Tomb No. 15 (Wiegand's numbering) leads into a tiny vestibule with nicely cut masonry showing traces of painting, from which steep stone steps descend to the long main spine of a hypogeum. The spine is crossed almost immediately by transepts of which, like the spine, there are several loculi housings (Fig. 141—plan ex Michalowski).

It is still possible to descend into some of these hypogea but others have been closed off. Nonetheless the view from ground level of an impressive flight of steps—already collecting the sand and debris again—plunging down to a sealed door, is in a way awe-inspiring. The fact that many of the ceilings of hypogea have collapsed allows one to peer into that which was once closed off (Fig. 142).

From the discovery of the relationship between tower tombs and hypogea the Polish team were able to postulate the idea that 'the dead were buried first in the underground part, and that use was made of the tower proper only after the former was full'.† It would appear that the combining of tower and hypogea never became wholly accepted as standard practice and in consequence we find that from the middle of the second century hypogea became practically the only type of sepulchre in Palmyra. This remained so until the city lost its independence in the third quarter of the third century.

* *Berytus*, Vol. 23, 1574.   † Michalowski, *Palmyra*.

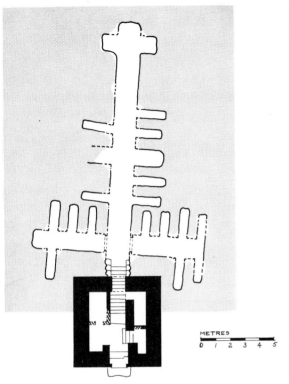

Fig. 141 Plan of Tower Tomb Hypogeum No. 15 (based on the plan published by Professor Michalowski).

Fig. 142 A collapsed hypogeum. The steps originally led down into the underground system.

From the sculptural detail and rich architectural treatment of these sepulchres it can only be assumed that they were those of the rich such as priests, city officials, army commanders and well-to-do merchants. The question arises as to where the common folk were buried for no major cemeteries have been found; this has led Professor Michalowski to suggest that use was made of abandoned tombs. However, for all their considerable number, there would hardly have been enough sepulchres to accommodate the steady supply of corpses even from a city with a diminishing population. It seems more likely that they were given a grave in the desert, perhaps marked by some kind of inscribed stelae like those which are now in the Palmyra Museum. The poorest would have been given an unmarked grave and left.

All about the hillsides are the yawning entrances to hypogea, some of them walled with well dressed stones (Fig. 143). These are mostly of the first century A.D. though everything cannot be attributed to this period. The sinister silence seems oppressive, and there is about the Valley of Tombs an air of death beyond death. It is as though the sun has bleached all colour from the after-life and left us with only academic interest and romanticism. In much the same way, remoteness in time and the science of history have reduced memory of the living and the dead to one and the same thing—objects of study and curiosity. We can feel no communion now with Julius Aurelius Bolma, son of Zabdibol; he is a name not a person, a carved title upon a tomb, an abstract. And yet in this valley with its wide, remote-seeming hills and its silence there is an intense feeling of the past. Bolma, Hairan, Elahbel and Banai and their companions crowd in on you, rattling the pebbles at your feet, haunting the still air, whispering in the wind an invitation to remember and resurrect. In the dying light of late evening they play havoc with the imagination.

A convenient track leads from the area of the Elahbel Tower Tomb, behind the bulk of the Gebel Umm el Belquis to one of the main water supplies of ancient

Fig. 143 An hypogeum on a hillside with a looted, sculptured sarcophagus lying beside the entrance.

Fig. 144 The ancient steps leading down to Ain Efqa.

Palmyra. A in E f q a lies alongside the modern road to Homs yet its sulphurous waters can be smelt from a considerable distance off.

Now, as in the past, it irrigates the whole oasis. Modern retaining walls protect the stream as it emerges from its walled-up grotto and make a nonsense of the flight of ancient steps which descend into the pungent waters (Fig. 144). Amid the vivid green of waterside vegetation are broken fragments of pillars and altars; some still even lie in the water. At the entrance to the grotto, which is today approached down a dank internal staircase, are several altars, one of which is dedicated to Zeus the Most High, Lord of the World. These were dedicated by Bolana, son of Zebida during the spring of A.D. 162, when he was *curator* of the spring. These altars were recovered in 1947, although one of them is recorded from the eighteenth century.

The word Efqa is Aramaic and means 'Issue of' (waters), and indeed this substantial stream does issue forth from the grotto in a most dramatic and unexpected way. Originally the mouth of the cavern was open and the water emerged from the dark interior instead of slipping under the modern wall. In fact

Fig. 145 The South-west Necropolis.

the grotto through which the stream flows extends back under the Gebel Muntar for some 600 metres (approximately 1,800 feet), and it is quite possible to wade upstream in the shallow, warm water for a considerable distance. The temperature never changes, summer or winter, remaining at a constant 33° centigrade. Nor does its flow vary, 'issuing forth' at a rate of 5,000 cubic metres per day. This is a substantial body of water and, with its healing properties as an additional bonus, it is hardly surprising that it became a place of veneration.

Today, Ain Efqa provides, despite its modern walls, a fascinating and beautiful point in Palmyra (Plate 2). The green palms from which the city took its Roman name provide a marvellous splash of colour against the drab colours of the desert and the related gold and creams of the ruins.

Farther south, about half a mile, is a group of tower tombs and hypogea known as the SOUTH-WEST NECROPOLIS (Fig. 145). As one approaches, one crosses the line of the first-century south wall and the remains of the original, outer gate. This is not to be confused with the so-called Damascus Gate close to Diocletian's Camp. The pavement is still visible in this gateway and shows deep ruts, ground out by the passing wheeled carts and chariots many hundreds of years ago.

The tower tombs of this area are of the first century A.D. and they display that transitional period between polygonal and dressed stone as exemplified by the Tower Tomb of Kithoth (Fig. 1) and the Elahbel Tower Tomb (Fig. 137). Here

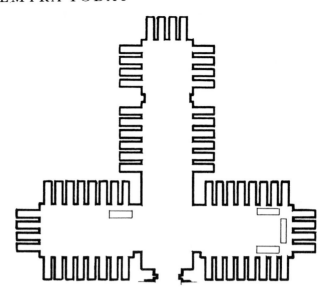

Fig. 146 The plan of the Hypogeum of
the Three Brothers.

METRES

0   5   10   15

the masonry is rough and yet it is laid in uneven courses. The towers rise,
agonisingly isolated amid a sea of rock-strewn tufts of grass, etched starkly across a
bare landscape like sentinels set down and then forgotten by the passing army of
time. Above, the faceless sky glares defiantly down on them.

However, it is not the tower tombs which are the highlight of this necropolis, but
the hypogea. The most important of these is known as the HYPOGEUM OF THE
THREE BROTHERS. The door to this family tomb is approached down a long,
modern ramp, and is a beautiful piece of carving. Richly decorated with architectural features, it is a delightfully balanced design. The great interest of the door lies
in the inscriptions carved upon it regardless of any architectural context, which
record that it was established by the three brothers, Malé, Saadai and Naamain in
the middle of the second century A.D. There is the placement for a lamp over the
door.

Through the heavy stone doors one enters, down a few steps, an inverted
T-shaped chamber. Basically there are three arms radiating from a focal point by
the door (Fig. 146), each with recesses on either side in which were placed six
loculi. There are sixty-five recesses in all, providing plentiful accommodation for
generations of the family. The vault and walls of the main arm are of brick covered
with painted plaster. The barrel vault is painted with a familiar pattern of
hexagons (Fig. 14) in blue with gilded rosettes and flowers. Here again one has an
example of that passionate love of geometric design which so fascinated Wood and

Dawkins. There is a large central circular panel in which is portrayed the Abduction of Ganymede. This was a favourite theme in Hellenistic times, in which the childishly pretty face of Ganymede was particularly favoured. The legend relates that he was the son of Tros of Troy, and was carried off by Zeus to be his cup-bearer. In recompense his father was given a breed of marvellous horses or, according to other ancient sources, a golden vine. The early sources of the story relate that Zeus wanted a handsome cup-bearer and, disguised as an eagle, descended and abducted Ganymede. In this version the eagle is equated with the constellation Aquilla, and Ganymede with Aquarius. As with all classical mythology, the form and content of the story vary according to date and source. The colouring has survived incredibly well and the state of these frescoes is remarkable.

At the end of the main arm are a series of frescoes in the Graeco-Syrian style dating from the early third century A.D. Once again we have that curious blend of styles, the Hellenistic and the Oriental combining to create something highly individual. As with the usual oriental, 'Parthian', tradition the figures are placed in frontal poses, creating a rather lifeless effect, yet there is a Hellenistic swirl to the draperies for all their stiffness. In the lunette at the top, framed by the vault, is a scene from the Iliad with Ulysses discovering Achilles, wearing women's clothing, amongst the daughters of Lycomedes, King of Scyros, where his mother had hidden him in a vain attempt to save her son from his fatal destiny. This theme is also portrayed in the mosaics in the Patrician Houses behind the Sanctuary of Bel (see page 99). It is interesting why this subject should have been popular with the Palmyrenes. Appropriate enough a theme in a tomb because Achilles is the symbol of the eternal soul. Robed in borrowed, earthbound clothes which are not natural to him, he sheds these at death and thus liberates his soul to the timeless life for which he was created. But as the pavement of a house it seems to be a little strange, indeed morbid. Was there then a consuming preoccupation with death and after-life in the Palmyrene psyche which ventured near to that of the Egyptians?

Round the base of the vault there is a delightfully clever trompe l'oeil cornice painted with a neat array of small dentils.

Between the stacks of loculi the walls have been frescoed in a most attractive way. Circular portrait medallions are carried by winged Victories who stand in a horribly uncomfortable position. This design has parallels in other places, notably at Dura-Europos where the design is a little freer in execution, not so solid in appearance, and in mosaics in the fifth-century Church of St Prassede in Rome. Also, the ninth-century mosaic interior of the Byzantine chapel of St Zeno, known as the 'Garden of Paradise', does have a stylistic resemblance to the Victories in the Three Brothers Tomb. The decay of the Hellenistic/Parthian culture left a rich compost which was to become a contributory factor in the seedbed stage of Byzantine art. With the spread of Byzantine culture, even in Italy with its then sterile traditions, ideas and decorative concepts were able to creep in from the most surprising and outlandish places.

The right arm of the hypogeum contains the substantial remains of three fine sarcophagi. Headless effigies recline, clustered together, holding cups, or just relaxing ceremoniously, on couches of the familiar type. Between the turned legs of the couches are a series of portrait busts. The sarcophagus of Malé is located in the left arm.

The importance of this extraordinary interior cannot be overrated for it brings together so much of what is typical in late Palmyrene art. Clearly shown is that curious juxtaposition of two, if not three, cultures, all being assimilated and yet remaining separate.

Nearby is another important hypogeum which contains some good sculptured sarcophagi. This is the HYPOGEUM OF ATENATAN which, from a text over the door, can be dated to A.D. 98. However, in A.D. 229 a man called MAQQAI added an exedra to the north. Maqqai's sarcophagus carries two portraits of himself, one very delightful one with two page-boys in attendance. One of the boys is holding his horse and the other his bow. These sculptures were painted, and originally the impact must have been quite startling. The costumes worn (see page 31) reflect the fashionable liking for Greek or Parthian styles rather than for the, perhaps, homespun trend of local Palmyrene attire. What is so fascinating about these sculptures is the handling and arrangement of the figures. Normally the figures are set in a line, all facing the front, stiff and rather lifeless. Here, however, the boys are actually attending Maqqai; there is an attempt at realism. The left-hand boy is half turned towards his master whilst the other, with the bow, looks away, perhaps spying out the field of sport. There is an intimacy, a feeling of an everyday event about it. The detailing is also clearly worked, a far remove from the stiffness and rigidity of earlier sculptures. This marks a move towards the Hellenistic approach, away from the Parthian, and yet the two influences are still distinct. The Abbé Starcky has pointed out that this development of stylistic forms reveals a 'distinctive feature of Oriental art (which) will again be quite conspicuous in Byzantine art'.

Also in the South-west Necropolis is the HYPOGEUM OF HAIRAN and another with fine frescoes depicting Dionysos. All these, and the now much ruined HYPOGEUM OF MALKO, can be visited by arrangement with the Department. The majority of these hypogea were excavated by Ingholt. Frescoes in varying states of preservation can be seen but those visitors with only a relatively short time to spare will see the best and most interesting in the Three Brothers Hypogeum and the Atenatan Hypogeum.

Before going to the South-east Necropolis, a short detour can be made to a prominent Honorific Column. It stands a short distance up the hill towards the

ruins from Ain Efqa, a solitary pillar against a background of palm trees. There were, as far as we know at present, four such HONORIFIC COLUMNS (Fig. 147, see page 169), and they originally carried a statue on the top. There is little to distinguish this from the one just east of the Baal Shamin Temple, and their purpose, to honour in a special way someone who had made a notable contribution to the fortunes of the city, was the same.

Southwards again, past Ain Efqa and the south-western necropolis, one turns off the main road and heads down a dust track to the SOUTH-EAST NECRO-POLIS. This is an area in which there are tens of hypogea of which three have been restored by the Department. Their discovery was almost by accident for in 1957, when the Iraq Petroleum Company were laying a pipeline (see page 75), they came across more than twenty hypogea. This of course presented enormous and immediate problems both to the Department and the Company. The laying of the pipeline was of high priority but against this the needs of archaeology were equally

Fig. 147 An honorific column near Ain Efqa.

Fig. 148 A stone door with its coffered panels which are typical of nearly all tombs in Palmyra.

important. The fact that the minimum of damage was done in this conflict of interests is encouraging. This has, however, led to one rather incongruous feature. The ditch which leads down to the entrance of the 'No 5' Hypogeum is spanned by a massive oil pipe.

HYPOGEUM No. 5 is referred to by its number due to the lack of any inscription relating to its *curator*. The doorway has the familiar stone doors panelled out with rectangular coffers (Fig. 148). The hinges are of bronze. Immediately inside is a well and beyond this is the main arm with four subordinate ones. There are sixty-five bays in all, each containing six loculi. The tomb was established in the late second century by the family of Artabn Zabdoun, son of Malko, son of Yarhai the priest of Aglibol and Malakbel. This much is known from an inscription over the shoulder of a bust of Artabn which can be seen on the right of the main arm. This arm is lined with stone, lightly 'engraved', whilst at the back is a sarcophagus and a representation of the sacred meals which were such a part of the cult of the dead. There is a charming touch in this carving which shows two little children presenting their father with garlands of flowers as he lies on his couch.

Next to No. 5 is the HYPOGEUM OF BOLHA, son of Nabo Shori. Over the lintel of the door there is an inscription dated A.D. 88. Much of the main arm was in a very poor state when the Department undertook restoration in 1958, but the two subordinate arms have been cleared as has most of the main section. This includes fifty-three bays, each with four recesses for loculi, separated by stone slabs and tiles.

Certain modifications were made by Bolha's sons and grandsons. The affairs of most families in Palmyra had their ups and downs, and this modest rearrangement was possibly due to the fortunes of the Shori family having taken a set-back. Merchant and other wealthy families who suddenly fell on hard times with no foreseeable recovery sold off their houses of eternity, or at least parts of them. The sarcophagi are good examples, as is the bust of the *curator* as a piece of Palmyrene portrait sculpture. In the third recess of the first bay of the main arm is another typical piece of sculpture. It is of Nibna, wife of Bolha, son of Zabad Bol.

Probably the most fascinating hypogeum in this area, and certainly the most grandiose architecturally, is the HYPOGEUM OF BREIKI, son of Zubaid. This is sometimes referred to as No. 9. It was excavated by the Department in 1958, following the 'exposures' by the Iraq Petroleum Company, and has been tactfully restored. Again, the doorway is closed by a single stone slab. But it is the architectural treatment of the interior which excites—comparable in some ways with the Yarhai interior—for there is a strong rhythm set up by enriched niches, arches, punctuated by Corinthian pilasters, with the whole composition tied together by a delicate cornice. For those who have seen the Yarhai interior in the Damascus Museum before reaching Palmyra, a visit to the Breiki Hypogeum is important because one sees *in situ* what the Yarhai really was like. The Yarhai is probably better architecture, more polished as a performance, but it suffers from having been truncated and particularly by having been taken out of context. Here one descends from the brilliant sunlight into the shadowy tomb with all the atmosphere, the tricks of light penetrating through the door.

To add to the air of mystery of this hypogeum, there are two doors which lead into other family vaults: the southern into that of the family Ilami, son of Aben—dated A.D. 108—and the northern into that of the family of Timamed, son of Malko—dated a little earlier, A.D. 93.

The various families of Palmyra who were in a position to rule must have been quite closely interrelated, for there is a constant cross-relation on names; so-and-so's son in one tomb also appears in an inscription in another. The concept of the family was obviously enormously strong.

From the South-east Necropolis it is possible to drive back into Palmyra along a track which goes through the palm groves and eventually comes out in the vincinity of the Sanctuary of Bel. This is a charming, though sometimes bumpy,

Fig. 149 The north city wall.

ride with the sunlight dappling through the trees, casting crazy patterns on the hard ground. After a day down sepulchres, commiserating with the dead, or just being stifled by them, it is refreshing to be bumped, bounced and bruised amid all that sunlit greenery, back into the fresh air of the living present.

Too little is known of the walls of the city for much to be said of them. The circuit has, however, been traced (Map 2) and it is obvious that it enclosed an enormous area. This raises the question as to whether it was a defensive wall, an agricultural enclosure containing the limits of the orchards and groves of the city's edge, or a Customs wall; the traces are today called locally the Sur el Jumrok (Customs limit). Isolated stretches of it have been excavated, and it is thought to be of the first century A.D.

The inner wall—known as Zenobia's Wall—encloses a much smaller area by comparison. An area, in fact, which only contained the principal civic structures and a concentrated residential area. This wall is well preserved on the northern side and is punctuated by a sequence of towers and bastions (Fig. 149). With the

211

Fig. 150 The western section of the north wall
rising up the hill above Diocletian's Camp.

rest of the inner wall this was altered and strengthened by the Byzantine Emperor
Justinian (A.D. 526–65) in an attempt to repair the damage done by the army of
Aurelian in A.D. 272. The northern wall is constructed with large blocks of stone
and is defensive in character. It dates in the main from the period of Odainat and
Zenobia. It curves in southwards at its western end, and use is here made of
existing tower and house bombs (see page 171) to serve as bastions. Just behind
the Funerary Temple it turns abruptly westwards and climbs the precipitous hill
behind the Camp of Diocletian (Fig. 150). It drops again having reached the
summit towards the south-east to join up with the Damascus Gate.

From here it runs eastwards and is in places incorporated into prominent

Fig. 151 The so-called 'Zenobia' wall.

buildings. There is an air of hasty construction here, with already existing stout walls of fine buildings being used to cut down the work to be done. It runs along the lip of a shallow wadi (Fig. 151), called the Wadi el Kubur, which would have added to its defensive potential.

Popular belief has it that the whole inner circuit, both north and south, was built by Zenobia when threatened by the advance of Aurelian. The northern section is, however, well and orderly made and is a good piece of military architecture. This suggests that this section was constructed before her revolt against Rome leaving only the southern part of the wall to be erected hastily when faced with disaster. This has not been confirmed by excavation and remains a point of conjecture.

PALMYRA

*

Remote in its desert fastness, Palmyra is one of the most romantic sites to have come down to us from the ancient world. It is the quintessence of a caravan city. The sheer beauty of the ruins, the monumental scale of the site and the buildings, the richness and sumptuousness of detail, all leave an indelible mark upon the mind. The strange, often bizarre cross-fertilisation of cultures is of absorbing interest, yet it is the ever changing light, the loneliness and the sense of departed glory which catches the imagination. One can visit the streets and spaces in pursuit of dispassionate academic knowledge—and there are rich rewards in this—but to succumb to the flood of beauty and romanticism is the best mood in which to appreciate Palmyra.

The Palmyrenes loved their city. Those who roam through its ruins today and delight in its splendour with the same satisfaction as Bolna or Yarhai, are as much a part of Palmyra as the ancient builders. Their response gives life to the Bride of the Desert.

Glossary of Architectural Terms

Acroteria Plinths for statues or sculptured ornaments placed above the three angles of a pediment; also, more loosely, both the plinth and what stands on it.

Adyton The inner sanctuary, holy of holies, reached from the cella of a temple.

Agora Large open place of public assembly.

Apse Vaulted semicircular or polygonal termination, usually to a chancel or chapel.

Architrave The lowest of the three main divisions of an Entablature; also, the moulded frame surrounding a door or window.

Cavea Semicircular auditorium of a theatre.

Cella The main body or room of a temple.

Coffers Sunken square or polygonal ornamental panels.

Cornice The top, projecting, section of an Entablature.

Crepidoma or **Crepis** The stepped outer edge of the platform of a temple.

Entablature The upper part of an Order, placed usually above and connecting columns, consisting of Cornice, Frieze and Architrave.

Exedra An open recess for sitting in.

Frieze The middle division of an Entablature, usually decorated but sometimes left plain.

Intercolumnation The space between two adjacent columns.

Nymphaeum Literally, a temple of the Nymphs, but applied to pleasurable places containing flowers, statues and, most particularly, fountains and pools of water.

Orchestra The paved, usually semicircular area, between the stage and the auditorium of a Roman theatre.

Pediment The low-pitched gable end to a classical building, delineated on all three sides by the cornice.

Peristyle Colonnade round the inside of a courtyard or room, but also used to describe the 'peripteral' colonnade round the outside of a structure.

Pilaster A shallow rectangular column attached to a wall and projecting only slightly from it.

Podium A platform on which a temple or other building stood.

Propylaea A stately entrance gate to a temple precinct or palace.

Pylon Correctly, a gateway, but more loosely a tall structure intended to demarcate or decorate.

Scaenae frons The wall at the back of the stage in a theatre, containing the principal entrances onto the stage.

Soffit The underside of an architectural element.

Temenos A sacred enclosure or precinct.

Triclinium A dining room, strictly with three couches.

Tesserae (**1**) Small squares of bone, moulded clay or other manufacture used as a token or ticket. (**2**) Small cubes of glass, stone or marble used in mosaic.

215

Bibliography

Ass'ad, K., and Taha, O., *Welcome to Palmyra*, Damascus, 1966

Bible, The—Old Testament

Cassas, L.-F., *Voyage Pittoresque de la Syrie etc.*, Paris, 1799

Chabot, J.-B., *Choix d'Inscriptions de Palmyre*, Paris, 1922

Champdor, A., *Les ruines de Palmyre*, Paris, 1953

Collart, P., and Vicari, J., *Le sanctuaire de Baalshamin à Palmyre*, Rome, 1969

Colledge, M. A. R., *The Art of Palmyra*, London, 1976

—, *Parthian Art*, London, 1977

Damascus Museum, *Guide de l'exposition des dernières découvertes classique en Syrie*, Damascus, 1969

Dawkins, J., and Wood, R., *The Ruins of Palmyra*, London, 1753

Dunant, C., *Le sanctuaire de Baalshamin à Palmyre*, Rome, 1971

Fedden, R., *Syria and Lebanon*, London, 1965

Fellmann, R., *Le sanctuaire de Baalshamin à Palmyre*, Rome, 1970

Février, J., *La réligion des Palmyreniens*, Paris, 1931

—, *Essai sur l'histoire politique et économique de Palmyre*, Paris, 1931

Frankfort, H., *The Art and Architecture of the Ancient Orient*, London, 1970

Halifax, W., *Report on a Voyage to Palmyra*, Philosophical Transactions of the Royal Society, London, 1695

Ingholt, H., *Palmyrene and Ganharan Sculpture*, New Haven, 1954

Irby, C. L., and Mangles, J., *Travels, etc.*, London, 1823

Koran, The

Lazareff, Prince A., *Palmyra*, St. Petersburg, 1884

Loos, C., *Den Första Svenska Orient-expeditionen, och C. Loos' teckningar*, Sweden, 1932

Lyttelton, M., *Baroque Architecture in Classical Antiquity*, London, 1974

Meryon, C. L., *The Travels of Lady Hester Stanhope*, London, 1846

Michalowski, K., *Palmyra*, London, 1970

Murray, S. B., *Hellenistic Architecture in Syria*, Princeton, 1917

Musil, A., *Palmyrena: A Topographical Itinerary*, New York, 1928

Pliny, *Natural History*

Rostovtzeff, M. J., *Caravan Cities*, Oxford, 1932

BIBLIOGRAPHY

Schlumberger, D., *La Palmyrène de Nord-Ouest*, Paris, 1951

Schröder, *Sitzungsberichte der Preussischen Akademie der Wissenschaften*, Berlin, 1884

Starcky, J., *Dictionnaire de la Bible*, Paris, 1957

Starcky, J., and Munajjed, Ṡ., *Palmyra*, Damascus, 1960

Stark, J. K., *Personal Names in Palmyrene Inscriptions*, Oxford, 1971

Summerson, Sir J., *Architecture in Britain 1530–1830*, London, 1969

Temporini, H. von, *Aufstieg und Niedergang der Antiken Welt*, Tübingen, 1977

Vogüé, M. de, *La Syrie Centrale*, Paris, 1865/77

Volney, C.-F., *Oeuvres complètes etc.*, Paris, 1821

Wiegand, T., *Palmyra, Ergebnisse der Expeditionen von 1902 und 1917*, Berlin, 1932

And articles and papers by the following: Bounni, A., Cantineau, J., Chabot, J. B., Clermont-Ganneau, C., Collart, P., Dunant, C., Gabriel, A., Ingholt, H., Michalowski, K., Schlumberger, D., Seyrig, H., Starcky, J., and others in the following publications: *Antiquités Syriennes, Annales Archéologiques de Syrie, Annales Archéologiques Arabes Syriennes, Berytus, Bulletin of the American Schools of Oriental Research, Fouilles Polonaises, Journal of Roman Studies, Palestine Exploration Quarterly, Revue Biblique, Syria*, and other journals of learned Societies.

Index

References to illustrations are given in italic figures

INDEX